Interactive Text

Grade 3

Itzelle Espino ☆

Mc
Graw
Hill
Education

Contents

Contents

CHAPTER 1

Adaptations in Land Environments

 What are adaptations, and how do they help living things survive?

Vocabulary

 **environment** all the living and nonliving things in a place

 **biome** a place with certain kinds of living and nonliving things

 **adaptation** a body part or way of acting that helps a living thing survive

 **desert** a place with hot, dry weather

 **migrate** to move from one place to another

 **grassland** a place with many grasses

 **forest** a place with many trees

 **mimicry** when one thing pretends to be another thing

 **arctic tundra** a cold place above the Arctic Circle

Where do living things live?

Living things live where they can meet their needs. A living thing's **environment** includes all the living and nonliving things in a place.

A **biome** is a place that has certain kinds of living and nonliving things. Deserts, forests, and grasslands are types of biomes.

A buffalo eats the grass in its biome.

Different biomes have different kinds of weather over time. Some biomes are cold and dry. Some are warm and wet. The soil, or ground covering, might also be different. It might be hard or soft, moist or dry.

This desert biome has a hot, dry climate.

✓ Quick Check

1. How might one biome be different from another?

_____

2. Describe the kinds of weather in your biome.

_____

How do plants get what they need?

Most plants need the same things to live. They need water, light, food, and carbon dioxide. Carbon dioxide is found in the air. They must get all these things in their environment.

Parts of a Plant

Stems carry water and food.

Roots get water and food.

Most plants have roots, stems, and leaves. Each part of a plant helps it to live. Roots get water and food from the ground. Stems carry food and water through the plant. Leaves get sunlight and carbon dioxide. Other parts, like flowers and seeds, help a plant make more plants.

✓ Quick Check

3. Which plant part takes things from the ground?

_____

4. Why might some plants need long roots?

_____

Leaves get sunlight and carbon dioxide.

Read a Diagram

This diagram shows the parts of a plant that help it live.

How do animals get what they need?

Animals also need certain things to live. They need water, food for energy, and oxygen from the air or water. They also need a place to stay safe.

An animal's parts help it to live in its environment. Legs or wings help it move. Teeth or beaks help it eat.

▲ A lion uses its tongue to get water.

When animals breathe, they take in oxygen. Many animals have lungs to get oxygen from the air. Fish use gills to get oxygen from water.

Other animal parts help keep them safe. They might also use their parts to help build homes and shelters. Birds use their beaks to build nests for shelter.

▲ Birds use nests for shelter.

gills

✔ Quick Check

5. What body parts help you eat?

_____

6. Circle the body part that helps a dog get oxygen.

    wing   tail   lungs   gill

What helps living things survive in their environment?

Living things live where they can meet their needs. A redwood tree needs a cool, wet environment with rich soil. A cactus needs a warm, dry environment with sandy soil.

Cactus

Redwood

✔ Quick Check

Circle the proper conditions for each plant in the chart below.

Plant	Temperature	Type of Soil	Amount of Moisture
7. Cactus	warm cool	rich sandy	dry damp
8. Redwood	warm cool	rich sandy	dry damp

Living things have adaptations to help them survive in an environment. An **adaptation** is a body part or a way of acting that helps a living thing survive. Plants might have long roots to reach water deep in the ground. Animals might have a certain way of finding food to eat.

A bear catches fish in a river for food.

✓ *Quick Check*

9. Look at the photo. What adaptations might help this bear catch fish?

_____

LOG ON ℮-Review Summaries and quizzes online @ **www.macmillanmh.com**

What is a desert?

A **desert** is a biome with warm, dry weather. The Sonoran Desert is the largest desert in North America. A desert gets less than 25 centimeters (10 inches) of rain each year. There may be one day with a lot of rain. Then months may pass with no rain at all.

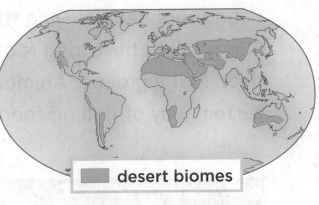

desert biomes

▲ **This map shows the locations of the deserts of the world.**

The Sonoran Desert

A desert can get very hot during the day. The Sun's heat warms the land and air. At night, the desert can cool off quickly.

Desert soil is mostly sand. Rain quickly drips through the sand. The water goes deeper than most plants' roots can reach.

✅ *Quick Check*

Tell whether each statement is true or false.

10. A desert gets more than 25 centimeters

of rain each year. _____

11. Plants in a desert biome have adaptations that

help them live with only a little water. _____

What adaptations help desert plants?

Desert plants have adaptations that help them get the water they need. Some plants have deep roots. These reach down into the ground for water. Other plants have shallow roots. These trap the water when rain falls.

Adaptations of Desert Plants

mesquite tree

Small leaves help save water.

Sharp thorns keep animals away.

Long roots reach deep underground.

saguaro cactus

Sharp spines keep animals away.

Thick, waxy stem helps store water.

Shallow roots trap water from rain.

Read a Diagram

These diagrams show adaptations in two different desert plants.

Desert plants have other adaptations that help them survive. Thick stems help them save water. Waxy skin helps seal in the water. Thorns and spines keep animals from eating the plants for food and water.

This aloe plant can grow in the desert. An aloe's waxy skin and thick leaves are adapted to store lots of water. ▶

 Quick Check

12. Use the graphic organizer below to compare the adaptations of the mesquite tree and saguaro cactus.

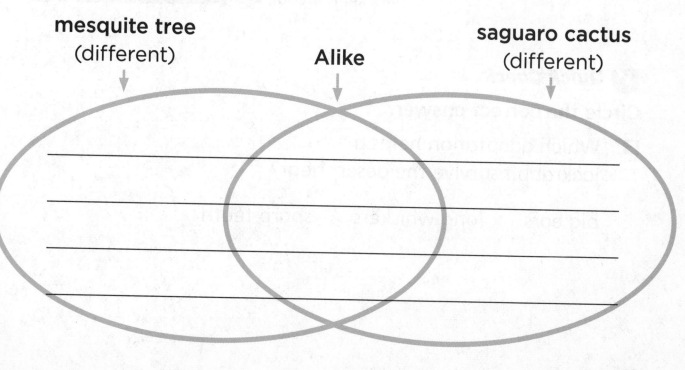

mesquite tree
(different)

Alike

saguaro cactus
(different)

What adaptations help animals?

Desert animals also have adaptations that help them survive in the heat. Some sleep during the hot part of the day. They come out at night when it is cool.

Rattlesnakes sleep during the day. ▶

Other animals have body parts that help them stay cool. A jackrabbit's big ears help it get rid of body heat. A thin body also helps it stay cool.

This jackrabbit's big ears keep it cool. ▶

✔ Quick Check

Circle the correct answer.

13. Which adaptation helps a jackrabbit survive the desert heat?

   big ears   long whiskers   sharp teeth

Some desert animals can be hard to see. Their bodies blend in with their environment. They can hide easily from other animals. This adaptation helps keep them safe.

▲ This frog can blend in with its environment.

✓ Quick Check

14. What might happen to the frog in the photo if it had bright green skin?

_____

What is a grassland?

A **grassland** is a biome with many grasses. It helps keep the land warm and moist. It gives animals a safe place to live and food to eat.

There are two kinds of grasslands. One has mild weather and four seasons. This grassland has rich soil that helps the grasses grow. The prairies of North America are an example of this type of grassland.

These grasslands in North America are called prairies.

Adaptations in Land Environments

The other type of grassland is warm all year long. These grasslands have a rainy season and a dry season. They also have trees and poor soil. During the dry season, these grasslands can dry out. They may catch fire.

These grasslands in Africa are called savannas.

 Quick Check

15. Use the graphic organizer below to compare the prairies and the savannas.

prairies (different)   **Alike**   **savannas** (different)

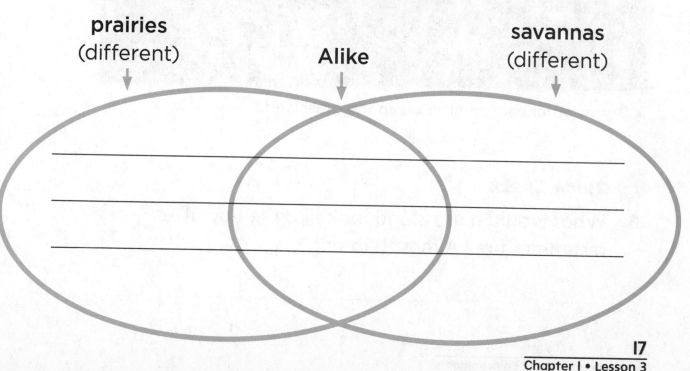

What adaptations help grassland plants survive?

Grassland grasses are adapted to dry weather. Most grasses have deep roots. This lets them get water from deep in the ground. If fire burns the part of the plant above the ground, the roots can grow new parts. This helps the grasses stay alive in the grassland.

▲ Dry weather can lead to fires in the grassland.

✓ Quick Check

16. What would a grassland look like the day after a summer fire? A month later?

_____

Trees in the grasslands also have adaptations that help them survive. The baobab tree only grows leaves in the wet season. It has a thick trunk to help it store water in the dry season. Its bark protects it against fire.

Adaptations help the baobab tree live in a grassland environment.

✔ Quick Check

17. Circle the adaptation that helps the baobab tree survive in the grassland.

thin bark   thick trunk   few roots

What adaptations help animals survive in grasslands?

Animals also have adaptations that help them live in the grasslands. Some have flat teeth to help them eat the grasses.

Others dig burrows, or holes, in the ground. This lets them hide from other animals. It also help's them stay cool in the heat.

A prairie dog can hide in a burrow.

A zebra's flat teeth can chew grass.

Some grassland animals can run very fast. This helps them catch other animals for food.

A cheetah can run fast to catch food.

 **Quick Check**

Tell how each adaptation below helps that animal survive.

18. A prairie dog digs a burrow.

_____

19. A zebra has flat teeth.

_____

20. A cheetah can run very fast.

_____

LOG ON **e-Review** Summaries and quizzes online @ **www.macmillanmh.com**

What is a forest?

A **forest** is a biome that has many trees. There are different kinds of forests in different places around the world.

Tropical rain forests can be found near the equator. Tropical rain forests are almost always hot and wet.

Tropical rain forests are dense and green. ▶

✔ *Quick Check*

21. Write a short weather forecast for a typical day in the rain forest.

_____

_____

A temperate forest has four seasons: spring, summer, fall, and winter. Summers are warm and wet. Winters can be cold and dry. These forests are found in North America, Europe, and Asia.

Temperate forests change from season to season.

✔ Quick Check

Fill in the blank.

22. In a _____ forest, it stays warm all year long.

What adaptations help forest plants survive?

Forest plants grow in layers. Plants in each layer have adapted to get the light and water they need to live.

In a tropical rain forest, tall trees have special roots that help keep them up. Some shorter plants have leaves with tips to get rid of extra water. Plants on the ground have large leaves that help them get sunlight.

Tropical Rain Forest

The tallest trees get the most light.

The next layer is formed by tree branches and leaves.

Trees in the middle layer don't get as much light.

The forest floor is dark and damp.

Read a Diagram

This diagram shows some of the layers in the rain forest.

There are two kinds of trees in a temperate forest. One kind has leaves that fall off when the seasons turn cool. The other stays green all year long. Both have adapted to survive the cold, dry winter.

This tree's leaves change color and drop off in the fall.

✓ Quick Check

Tell whether each statement is true or false.

23. Plants on the ground in the rain forest get a lot of sunlight. _____

24. Some trees in a temperate forest have no leaves in the winter. _____

How do animals survive in a tropical rain forest?

Tropical rain forests have more kinds of animals than anywhere else. Their adaptations help them stay safe.

Some bright, colorful animals use poison to stay safe. Their color warns other animals to stay away. An animal that attacks might get poisoned.

This frog's colors warn that it may be poisonous.

Some animals in tropical rain forests can run fast to get away from danger. Others climb high in the trees, or fly to be safe.

Mimicry is when one thing pretends to be another thing. Some animals use mimicry to blend in with their environment. The color and body shape of a mantis make it look like a flower.

▲ This mantis looks like a flower and is hard to see. To find the mantis, look for its head.

✔ Quick Check

Tell how each adaptation below helps forest animals.

25. colors that stand out

_____

26. colors that blend in

_____

How do animals survive in a temperate forest?

Animals in the temperate forest need to survive cold weather. Their adaptations help them. Some grow heavy coats in winter to stay warm. Some eat more or store food for the winter. Others sleep through the coldest months.

▲ **This dormouse sleeps through the winter.**

Animals in the temperate forest need to stay safe. Their adaptations helps them survive.

A skunk can spray other animals. The spray smells and stings their eyes.

A porcupine has many sharp quills. These can hurt an animal that tries to attack. Most animals will leave the porcupine alone.

▲ This porcupine's quills help keep it safe.

This skunk can spray other animals. ▼

Quick Check

27. What adaptation makes sure an animal has enough food in the winter?

What is an arctic tundra?

The **arctic tundra** is a cold biome above the Arctic Circle. Winters are long, dark, and very cold. Few plants and animals can be found.

In the middle of winter, the Sun never rises. In the middle of summer, the Sun never sets.

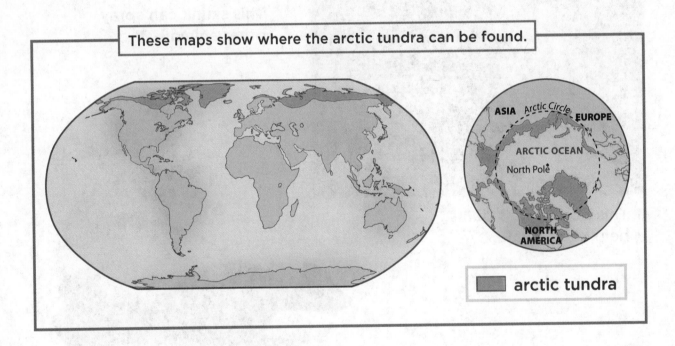

These maps show where the arctic tundra can be found.

arctic tundra

The arctic tundra has a short but beautiful summer.

Part of the tundra stays frozen all year long. Snow on top of the ground may melt in the summer. The water cannot soak into the ground. Puddles and pools of water form on top.

Small plants grow on the tundra in summer. Animals come back to the tundra to eat the plants. Some build nests in the plants.

✔ Quick Check

Circle the correct answer.

28. In which direction is the Arctic tundra located?

north   south   east   west

What adaptations help arctic plants?

Arctic plants have adaptations that help them survive. Their roots stay close to the top of the ground. This helps them get water. Some arctic plants have no roots at all.

Arctic plants stay short and small. This protects them from the cold and the wind.

lichen

Lichen stay short and cling to rocks.

Many plants on the tundra grow in clumps. This protects them from the wind and cold.

The dark colors of arctic flowers also helps the plants. They attract animals that can help spread seeds. This lets new plants grow.

The dark flowers of the dwarf fireweed help it get sunlight.

✓ **Quick Check**

Fill in the blank.

29. Most arctic flowers have a

_____ color.

What adaptations help arctic animals?

Arctic animals have adaptations that help them stay warm. Some have small legs and arms to keep them from losing heat. Some have heavy fur that protects them from the cold. A thick layer of fat keeps their bodies warm.

This polar bear has adaptations that keep it warm.

✓ Quick Check

30. Why would a polar bear in the tundra have a larger body than a black bear in the forest?

Other adaptations help arctic animals move on snow and ice. Some have wide feet. This helps them stay on top of the snow. Sharp claws keep them from slipping on ice.

This lynx has thick fur and wide feet.

 **Quick Check**

31. How are snowshoes like an arctic animal's adaptation?

_____

What are some other arctic animal adaptations?

Many arctic animals **migrate** each year. They move from one place to another. Caribou, tundra swans, and Canadian geese are examples.

These animals can not survive the bitter cold winters. So they migrate south where it is warmer, and where they can find food.

The arctic tundra will get warmer in spring. Plants will grow again. Animals that migrated south will return.

▲ **Animals such as the caribou migrate each year.**

Adaptations in Land Environments

Some arctic animals change color with the seasons. The arctic hare and fox are examples. This adaptation helps them blend in with their environment. It keeps them safe from other animals.

arctic fox in summer

arctic fox in winter

✓ Quick Check

32. Explain how the white fur of the arctic fox keeps it safe in the winter.

_____

LOG ON ⓔ-Review Summaries and quizzes online @ **www.macmillanmh.com**

Use the words from the word box to fill in the blanks below.

environment	biome	adaptation
desert	grassland	forest
mimicry	tundra	migrate

1. A(n) _____ has certain
kinds of living and nonliving things.

2. Animals that _____
move from one place to another.

3. A(n) _____ includes
all the living and nonliving things in a place.

4. A(n) _____ has many trees.

5. _____ lets one
animal look like another animal or plant.

6. A(n) _____ is a biome
with many grasses.

7. A thick coat is a(n) _____
that helps an animal survive cold weather.

8. The arctic _____ is a
cold biome in the far north.

9. A(n) _____ has hot, dry weather.

CHAPTER 2

Adaptations in Water Environments

 What adaptations help living things survive under water?

Vocabulary

 **salt water** an environment that has water with salt in it

 **algae** tiny plantlike living things

 **fresh water** an environment that has water with no salt in it

 **gills** a body part that lets some animals (such as fish) breathe in water

 **ocean** a large body of salt water

 **wetland** a place where water covers the ground most of the year

What is a water environment?

Almost three quarters of Earth is covered by water. Environments that are mostly water have many names. They include ponds, lakes, rivers, streams, oceans, and seas.

✔ Quick Check

Circle the correct answer.

I. Which of the following is NOT a water environment?

lake   pond   (desert)   river

Earth's Water

= salt water (970 buckets)

= fresh water in rivers, lakes, streams and ponds (3 buckets)

= fresh water in ice and underground sources (27 buckets)

Freshwater environments have water that has almost no salt. These include lakes, ponds, and rivers.

In **saltwater** environments, the water contains salt. Oceans and seas are large bodies of water with salt in them.

Some special kinds of environments may have a mix of both fresh and salt water.

✓ Quick Check

2. Look at the diagram. What kind of water environment is most common on Earth?

Sai¹t water

Read a Diagram

This diagram compares the amount of fresh water and salt water on Earth.

Good Water

How are water environments different from each other?

Water environments have different amounts of salt in the water. They differ in other ways, too.

Some are shallow and have lots of light. Others are so deep that light cannot reach them. Plants and animals have a hard time living in very deep water.

✓ Quick Check

Fill in the blank.

3. Plants have a hard time getting light in

   _____deep_____ water.

▲ You can see many plants and animals in shallow water.

Adaptations in Water Environments

Water environments have different temperatures, too. Near the equator, the water is normally warm all year. In the far north and far south, it can be very cold.

Deep water can also be very cold. The Sun heats up water on the surface. In deep water where it is dark, the water stays cold.

✅ Quick Check

4. Describe how light and temperature are related in water environments.

Warm water is on the surface, and cold water

Scientists studying the ocean stay warm and dry in submarines.

What plants and animals live in water environments?

As you know, different kinds of land plants and animals have different needs. This is also true in water environments.

◀ This water lily grows in freshwater ponds.

Water lilies stay on top of fresh water to get light. Air in their leaves helps them float.

◀ These tropical fish stay in shallow salt water.

Most tropical fishes live in shallow salt water near the equator. They need to stay where it is light and warm to survive.

Some plants and animals have adapted to live in colder and darker water. For example, whales have a layer of fat that keeps them warm in cold water.

◀ These whales can swim deep in the ocean.

 Quick Check

5. Use the diagram below to compare the environments of tropical fish and whales.

tropical fish
(different)

Alike

whales
(different)

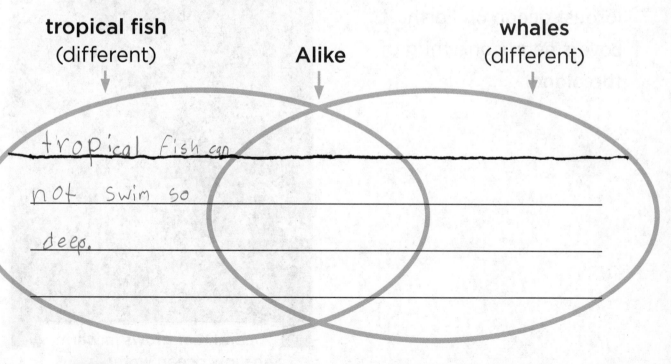

tropical fish can not swim so deep.

LOG ON **e-Review** Summaries and quizzes online @ **www.macmillanmh.com**

What is an ocean like?

An **ocean** is a large body of salt water.
There are five oceans on Earth:

- Atlantic
- Pacific
- Indian
- Arctic
- Southern

All of Earth's oceans are
connected to one another.

The Pacific Ocean is the
largest ocean on Earth. It
covers nearly one third of
the planet.

A coral reef grows in warm,
shallow ocean water.

Oceans contain billions of living things. Most of them live where the water is shallow and warm. This is true of the coral reef. The plants and animals in these colorful areas need warm water and lots of light.

This leafy sea dragon lives in the Southern Ocean near Australia.

✔ Quick Check

Tell whether each statement is true or false.

6. Most ocean plants and animals live in

deep water. _False_

7. The Pacific Ocean is the largest body of

water on Earth. _true_

How do plants survive in the ocean?

Most plants cannot survive in salt water. Eelgrass can. It has adapted to live in this environment.

Most of what looks like ocean plants are actually living things called **algae**. Like plants, algae needs water, sunlight, and carbon dioxide gas to live. Some algae have rootlike structures and attach to the ocean floor. Other kinds float near the water's surface.

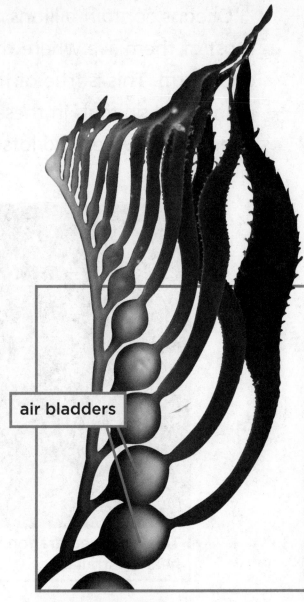

air bladders

▲ The air bladders in kelp help it float.

Eelgrass is a plant that lives in the ocean.

Kelp is a kind of algae found in the ocean. Kelp grows in groups called forests. They have parts like leaves that take in sunlight. Adaptations called air bladders help these leaves float in the water.

▲ Kelp is a kind of plant-like algae that lives in the ocean.

✔ Quick Check

8. What is the major difference between eelgrass and kelp?

Their both plants and are both in the ocen

How do animals survive under water?

Fish are the most common animal in the ocean. They have adaptations that help them live under water.

Fish breathe using **gills**. Gills are body parts that get oxygen from water.

Other body parts help a fish move through water. The shape of their bodies helps them swim quickly. Their fins and tails help them get where they need to go.

Read a Photo

This photo shows the location of a fish's gills ❶, fins ❷, and tail ❸.

Other adaptations help keep ocean animals safe. Some have sharp or poisonous parts. These can hurt or kill other animals. Others have colors that let them blend in with their environment.

This stingray has a sharp, poisonous tail.

✅ *Quick Check*

Fill in the blanks.

9. A green fish can ___blend in___ with green plants in its environment.

10. A fish uses its ___gills___ to get oxygen from the water.

How do animals survive in the very deep ocean?

The deep parts of the ocean are very dark and cold. Few plants and animals can live here. They need special adaptations to survive.

Some fish in the deep ocean have big eyes. This adaptation helps them see in the dark water.

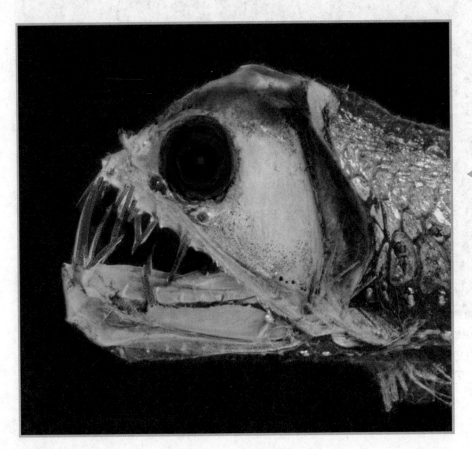

◀ The viperfish has large eyes.

✓ Quick Check

II. Why do some animals in dark environments have large eyes?

to help them see better

Other animals in deep water have parts that light up. This helps them see in the dark. The angler fish shown here is an example. Other fish might see the light and swim nearby. If they do, the angler fish might attack and eat them.

▲ The angler fish has a body part that looks like a fishing pole with a light on the end.

✔ Quick Check

12. How does an angler fish catch food in the deep ocean?

Because the fish can't see.

 **e-Review** Summaries and quizzes online @ www.macmillanmh.com

What are wetlands?

Wetlands are environments where water covers the ground most of the time. The water in wetlands can be salt water, fresh water, or a mix of both. Most of them are found where land and water meet.

The ground in wetlands does not hold much air. Plants need special adaptations to get what they need to survive.

The Florida Everglades are an example of wetlands.

The ground and plants in the wetlands can soak up a lot of water. This can help keep the area from flooding.

Wetlands can also take dirt and other things out of the water. The plants and ground act like a filter. This leaves the environment cleaner and safer for living things.

Wetlands Help the Environment

Read a Diagram

How do wetlands clean the environment?

 *Science in Motion* Watch how wetlands clean the environment @ **www.macmillanmh.com**

✔ *Quick Check*

Circle the letter of the correct answer.

13. Wetlands can act like a water filter to leave the environment _____.

   A. cleaner   **C.** darker

   B. colder   **D.** dirtier

What kinds of plants live in wetlands?

There are three main kinds of wetlands.

1. Marshes have grasses and reeds. There are no trees.

2. Swamps have trees and shrubs.

3. Bogs have moss and rich soil. Moss is a small, leafy plant.

a marsh

a swamp

a bog

Adaptations in Water Environments

Plants in the wetlands have adaptations to help them survive. Some have special tubes in their stems. These can carry oxygen down into the roots.

Mangrove tree roots can grow above the water. A mangrove seed can float for a long time. When it finds land, a new plant can grow.

A mangrove's roots can get what it needs from the air.

✔ *Quick Check*

Draw a line between the plants named and the type of wetland where you might find it.

14. moss   swamp

15. mangrove trees   marsh

16. grasses and reeds   bog

What kinds of animals live in wetlands?

Many kinds of animals live in the wetlands. Their adaptations help them find food, water, and shelter.

Some animals can spend time both on land and in water. Frogs are an example. A frog's skin can help it breathe in wet environments.

Wetland birds can stand still on their long legs in water. Their beaks help them catch fish and other small animals.

▲ This frog can spend time on land and in water.

These birds have adaptations that help them live in the wetlands.

In some wetlands, the environment changes over time. Animals may need to move to find water.

Some fish have fins like legs. The walking catfish is an example. It can move across land. Another body part helps it hold enough air to survive the short trip.

◀ This catfish can take a short walk on land.

✓ **Quick Check**

17. How are ~~frogs~~ *Frogs* and walking catfish alike in their adaptations?

they both live in the ocaen.

LOG ON **e-Review** Summaries and quizzes online @ **www.macmillanmh.com**

Water, Water, Everywhere!
Word Search

Find the words from the box in the word search.
Words can run up, down, and across. Then work
with a partner to define each word.

algae	freshwater	ocean	sea
bog	gills	pond	stream
creek	lake	river	wetland
fish	marsh	saltwater	

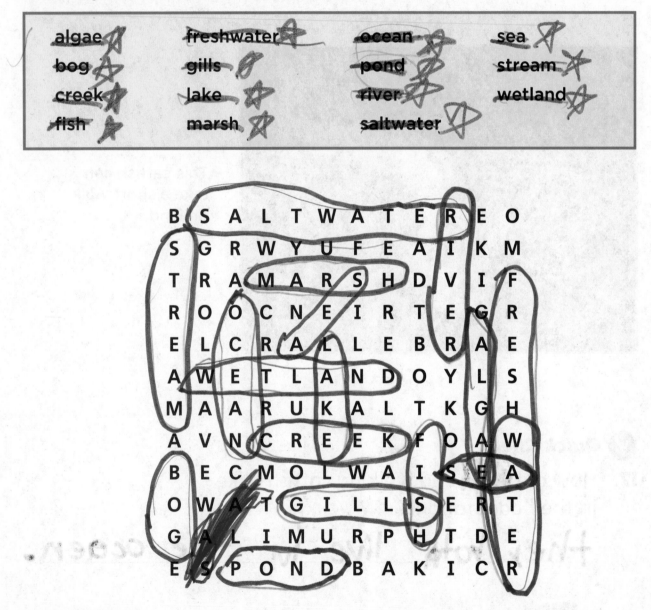

```
B S A L T W A T E R E O
S G R W Y U F E A I K M
T R A M A R S H D V I F
R O O C N E I R T E G R
E L C R A L L E B R A E
A W E T L A N D O Y L S
M A A R U K A L T K G H
A V N C R E E K F O A W
B E C M O L W A I S E A
O W A T G I L L S E R T
G A L I M U R P H T D E
E S P O N D B A K I C R
```

CHAPTER 3

Environments Change

The Big Idea How do changes to environments affect living things?

Vocabulary

pollution harmful things getting into the air, water, or land

reduce to use less of something

reuse to use something again

recycle to turn an old thing into something new

habitat the place where a living thing makes its home

extinct all dead, no more of that living thing alive on Earth

fossil the hardened remains of a living thing

Itzel is a person.

How do living things change their environment?

Living things make changes to their environments. Some changes are small. A bird might make a nest. Other changes can be large. Living things might break down a fallen tree. This can make the ground a better place for new plants.

The Environment Changes

Small plants grow in a bare environment.

Other living things come to use the plants for food and shelter.

Plants and animals compete with one another to get what they need. They all try to get food, water, sunlight, and shelter in the same place. If some cannot get what they need, they will die. Environments can change as living things compete to meet their needs.

 Quick Check

I. What might happen to a plant if its sunlight is blocked?

It will die if in doesnt,

Larger plants begin to grow. More animals come to get food and shelter.

In time, trees grow and things change even more.

Read a Diagram

How does this environment change over time?

LOG ON *Science in Motion* Watch how environments change @ www.macmillanmh.com

How does a beaver change its environment?

Beavers make many changes to their environment. They use their strong teeth to cut down trees and plants. They build dams across streams. This stops the water from flowing and makes a pool or pond. The beavers then build homes in the water.

Beavers use fallen trees, branches, and mud to build their dams and homes.

✓ Quick Check

2. What adaptation of beavers helps them to take down trees?

_____

Beaver dams cause big changes to the environment. Dry land behind the dam floods with water. The dam might stop water from flowing to other places. Plants may die, and other animals may have to move to get what they need.

Some changes might be good. Fallen trees might make room for more plants to grow. Wetlands may form and attract new living things.

▲ A beaver dam can turn a running stream into a deep pool of water.

 Quick Check

3. Use the diagram below to tell how a beaver dam can cause both good and bad effects.

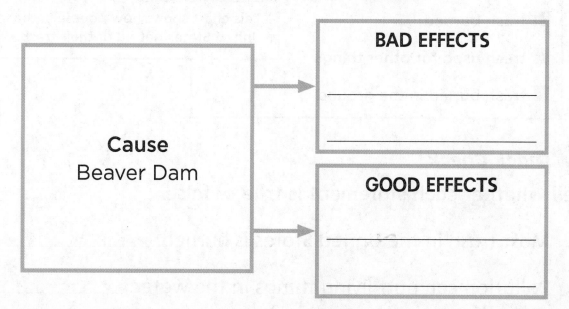

Cause
Beaver Dam

BAD EFFECTS
_____

_____

GOOD EFFECTS
_____

_____

How do people change their environment?

People make more changes to the environment than any other living thing. Some changes can be good. Others can be harmful.

People make a lot of trash. Some of this trash can get into the environment. This is called **pollution**. It can harm the living things of the land, water, and air.

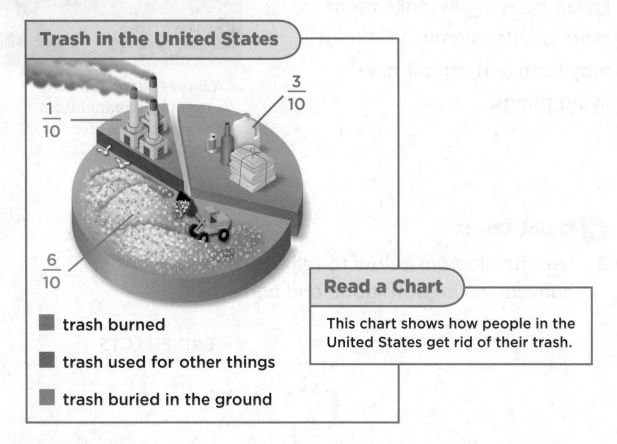

Trash in the United States

$\frac{1}{10}$

$\frac{3}{10}$

$\frac{6}{10}$

■ trash burned

■ trash used for other things

■ trash buried in the ground

Read a Chart

This chart shows how people in the United States get rid of their trash.

✓ Quick Check

Tell whether each statement is true or false

4. Most trash in the United States is burned. ___False___

5. Pollution can hurt living things in the water. ___Hure___

People can practice these "3 Rs" to cut back on trash and pollution.

reduce: use less of something

reuse: use things more than once

recycle: make new things out of old things

These acts will help us keep our environment healthy.

The things in this recycling bin can be used to make other products. ▶

 **Quick Check**

6. Write about a way in which people can help the environment. by recycleing and throwing away trash.

What are some ways environments change?

Weather can change an environment. Rain can make plants grow and blossom. Too much rain can cause floods. Not enough rain can turn green plants brown. Lightning can start fires in a dry grassland or forest.

Some changes last only a short time. Some last much longer. Earthquakes, storms, and volcanic eruptions can make sudden changes. These changes might last for years.

Too much rain caused a flood in this field.

Some living things recover quickly from environmental changes. Grassland grasses might come back soon after a fire. But trees may take many years to grow back.

Some changes can last forever. People may cut down all the trees in a place to build roads. Pollution in rivers and lakes can be lasting.

Plants start to grow again after a volcanic eruption.

✔ Quick Check

7. What change in the environment might result from too much rain? _A flood, lighting._

How do changes affect plants and animals?

A **habitat** is a living thing's home. Changes to a habitat can hurt the living things there. Their water might dry up. Food might become hard to find. Their adaptations may not help them survive big changes.

Some living things may need to find a new place to live. Others may need to find new ways to live. Those that cannot move or change their ways might die.

This animal depends on water found in its habitat. ▶

During a dry spell, water in the savanna might dry up. Some animals would need to move to find new water. Others might dig down into the ground and wait there for rain.

Plants cannot move when their habitats change. They might die. Animals such as fish might also die if their habitat dries up.

These elephants must move to find food and water when the weather stays dry.

 Quick Check

8. What might happen to an animal's habitat if no rain fell for many months? they can die if they don't have any water.

Grasses have enough light and water to grow.

Prairie dogs and other animals eat the grasses. Some animals eat other animals.

How do living things depend on each other?

Living things may depend on each other for their needs. Many animals use plants for food, water, and shelter. Some animals eat other animals. They may all share the same habitat.

Change may happen to one part of the habitat. One living thing might be harmed. That could lead to other changes in the habitat. All the living things in an environment are linked together.

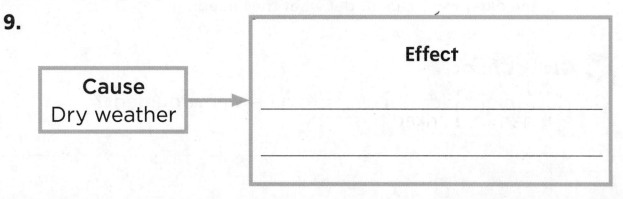

A dry spell might kill the grass. Prairie dogs would have no food.

If prairie dogs went away, other animals might need to move.

Read a Diagram

This diagram shows how change affects all the living things on the prairie.

Prairie dogs eat the grasses in their habitat. They dig burrows to stay safe. Other animals may use these burrows. Big animals eat the smaller animals. If the small animals went away, the whole environment would change.

 **Quick Check**

Use the graphic organizer below to list two effects of dry weather on the prairie.

9.

Cause
Dry weather →

Effect
_____

_____

What happens when new living things move in?

   Living things sometimes move from one environment into another. Animals might move to find new sources of food and water. Seeds from plants might blow on the wind or float down a river. People can also bring new plants and animals into a new place.

▲ People planted a new kind of tree here. Now the older trees cannot get what they need.

 Quick Check

10. How might plants move into a new environment?

<u>old people can plant them.</u>

New plants and animals can cause changes in an environment. They will use food and water that other plants and animals need. They might also bring sickness with them.

People once raised foxes for their fur. Then they let them go. Now the foxes try to get the same food and water as other animals in the wild.

This fox competes with other animals for food and space.

✓ **Quick Check**

11. How might a new kind of illness get from one place to another? Sometimes animals can carry the sickness.

LOG ON ⓔ-Review Summaries and quizzes online @ www.macmillanmh.com

What can happen if the environment suddenly changes?

Thousands of years ago, ice covered much of the United States. Then it grew warmer. The ice melted and some plants and animals could not survive in the warmer environment.

They became **extinct** over time. Extinct means there are no more left alive.

▲ This woolly mammoth became extinct when its environment grew warmer.

Some plants and animals become extinct due to changes in weather patterns. Others may die off from sickness. The things people do to an environment can make some living things extinct.

Responding to Change

Change	Living Thing	What Might Happen	Why
warmer climate	 saber-toothed cat	becomes extinct	unable to find food; unable to survive in warm climate
volcanic eruption	 short-tailed albatross	survives	flies to new environment
colder climate	 bear	survives	grows thicker fur

Read a Chart

This chart shows how changes might affect living things.

✔ Quick Check

Fill in the blank to complete each statement.

12. Over time, mammoths died off and became

_____.

13. The polar bear grew _____ fur as its environment got colder.

How can we learn about things that lived long ago?

Fossils are the hardened remains of things that were once alive. They teach us about living things from long ago. Some fossils can show us the size and shape of a plant or animal.

Fossils of teeth can tell us what an animal ate. Animals with sharp teeth could eat meat. Animals with flat teeth ate plants.

Fossils of bones can tell us how an animal moved. Foot and leg bones show if the animal could run or climb. Wing bones tell that an animal could fly.

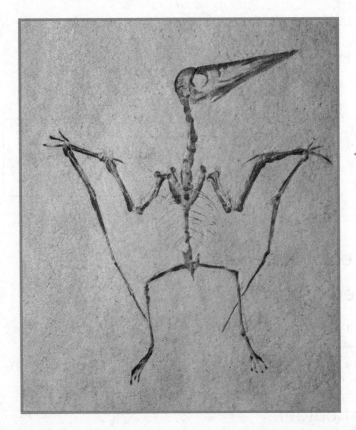

◄ This fossil shows an animal that had wings like a bird.

Fossils can also tell how Earth has changed. Some fossils of fish are found on land. This tells us that water covered that land long ago.

Layers of rock tell about Earth's history. Fossils found deep in the ground are the remains of the oldest plants and animals.

A fish fossil can tell us where oceans used to be.

✓ Quick Check

Draw a line between the kind of fossil and what it tells us.

14. flat teeth   animal could fly

15. wing bones   animal ate meat

16. sharp teeth   animal ate plants

How are living things today similar to those that lived long ago?

Some extinct animals are like animals of today. Woolly mammoths were like elephants. They were big and had tusks. They lived in groups. They had flat teeth and ate plants.

Mammoths were much bigger than elephants, though. Their tusks were much longer. They had thick hair and lived in cold habitats.

The woolly mammoth and the elephant look similar. ▶

woolly mammoth

elephant

Some dinosaurs of the past looked like lizards today. They had similar body parts. Maybe they used these body parts the same way, too.

Fossils can tell us if the animals ate the same foods. They can also tell if the animals moved the same way.

The dilophosaurus dinosaur (left) looked like the frilled lizard of today.

✓ Quick Check

Tell whether each body part belonged to a mammoth, to an elephant, or to both.

17. flat teeth _____

18. thick hair _____

Have some animals stayed the same over time?

Some animals have adaptations that work well over time. They can survive great changes in their environments. Fossils of such animals look almost the same as the animals today.

The fossil of a crocodile from long ago

a crocodile today

Shrimp survived when salt levels changed in the oceans. They have been nearly the same for over 100 million years. The cockroach is an example of an insect that has stayed about the same for millions of years.

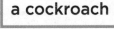

a cockroach

a shrimp

✅ Quick Check

19. Why might you compare a fossil from long ago to a living thing today? _____

_____

20. How are shrimp, crocodiles, and cockroaches different from most other living things? _____

_____

Rearrange the letters to form vocabulary words. Then write the word's number after its definition below.

1. t e x t n i c   __ __ __ __ __ __ __

2. e s u r e   __ __ __ __ __

3. t h a t i b a   __ __ __ __ __ __ __

4. c r e l e c y   __ __ __ __ __ __ __

5. l o f s i s   __ __ __ __ __ __

6. l i p o l o t u n   __ __ __ __ __ __ __ __ __

7. c e r u d e   __ __ __ __ __ __

a. the hardened remains of a living thing _____

b. to use less of something _____

c. harmful things getting into the air, water, or land _____

d. all dead, no more of that living thing alive on Earth _____

e. to use something again _____

f. the place where a living thing makes its home _____

g. to turn an old thing into something new _____

CHAPTER 4

Our Earth, Sun, and Moon

 The Big Idea How do Earth and the Moon move through space?

Vocabulary

 **rotate** to turn

 **orbit** the path an object takes as it moves around another object

 **axis** a line through the center of a spinning object

 **phase** the shape of the moon that we see

 **revolve** to move around another object

 **lunar cycle** the time it takes the Moon to go through all of its phases

How does the Sun's position in the sky seem to change?

The Sun seems to rise in the east each morning. It appears higher and higher in the sky. At midday it is high overhead. Then it appears to sink in the west. The Sun appears to set in the west at the end of the day.

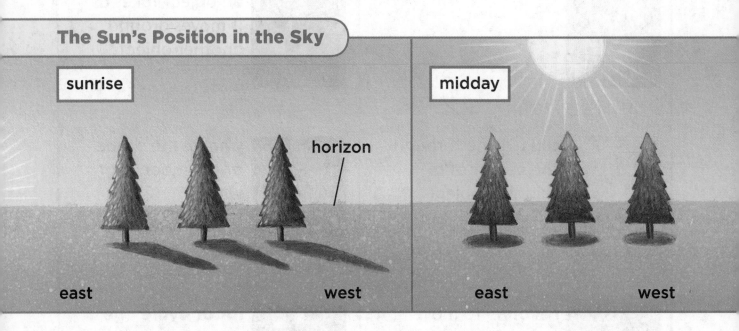

The Sun's Position in the Sky

sunrise

horizon

east

west

midday

east

west

✓ *Quick Check*

I. How does the position of the Sun seem to change during the day?

Shadows change with the position of the Sun in the sky.

Sunlight at midday comes down from high above. Shadows are very short. At sunrise, light comes in at a low angle. Shadows are long and stretch to the west. At sunset, shadows are long and stretch to the east.

▲ Shadows grow longer as the Sun sets.

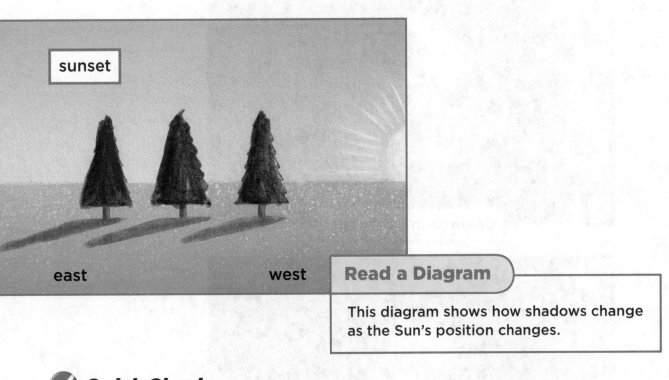

sunset

east   west

Read a Diagram

This diagram shows how shadows change as the Sun's position changes.

✔ Quick Check

Circle the best answer to complete the sentence.

2. At midday, your shadow will be _____.

    short   long   stretched

What causes night and day?

Our planet Earth is always moving. It **rotates**, or turns. It takes 24 hours, or one full day, to make one turn.

As Earth rotates, one side faces the Sun. It is daytime on that side. The other side faces away from the Sun. It is nighttime on that side.

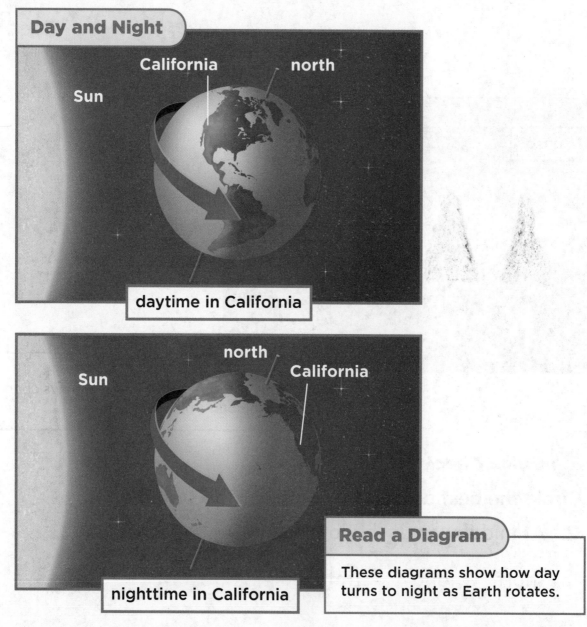

Day and Night

California   north

Sun

daytime in California

north

Sun   California

nighttime in California

Read a Diagram

These diagrams show how day turns to night as Earth rotates.

As Earth turns in space, the Sun seems to move. Earth rotates from west to east. This makes the Sun seem to move from east to west.

▲ The Sun rises to the east behind this tree. It will rise again in 24 hours.

✓ **Quick Check**

Fill in the blanks to complete each statement.

3. Earth rotates from _____

to _____.

4. The Sun seems to move from _____

to _____.

5. One day on Earth equals _____ hours.

What is an axis?

A ball can spin on your fingertip. It spins around an **axis**. An axis is a line through the center of a spinning object. The ball's axis starts at your fingertip. It goes to the top of the ball.

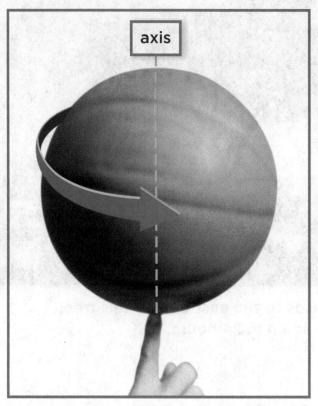

axis

▲ A ball spins around its axis.

✔ Quick Check

Circle the letter of the correct answer.

6. A spinning ball's axis goes _____.

   A. around the ball

   B. from inside to outside

   C. from top to bottom

   D. from side to side

Earth is shaped like a ball. It also has an axis. It rotates around this line. Earth's axis is tilted. It is not straight up and down.

The North Pole is at the north end of Earth's axis. The South Pole is at the south end.

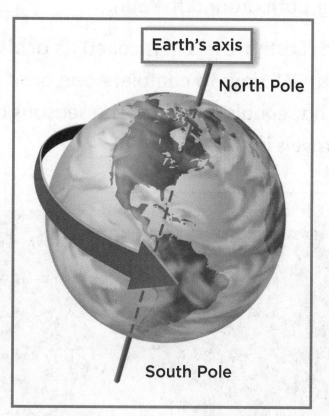

Earth's axis

North Pole

South Pole

▲ Earth's axis is slightly tilted.

 Quick Check

7. Describe Earth's axis.

_____

_____

LOG ON **e-Review** Summaries and quizzes online @ **www.macmillanmh.com**

Why do seasons change?

Earth does not just rotate in space. It also **revolves** around the Sun. This means it travels in a big circular path around the Sun.

The path Earth travels in is called its **orbit**. Earth takes about 365 days to complete one orbit around the Sun. That equals one year. The seasons change as Earth travels in this orbit.

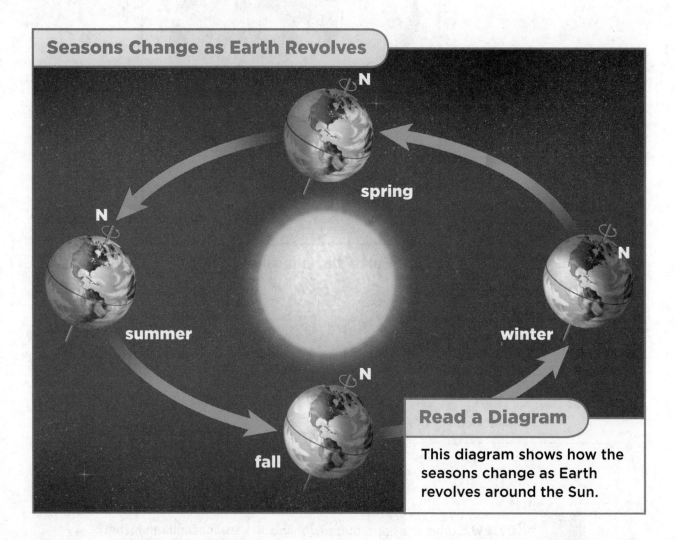

Seasons Change as Earth Revolves

N

spring

N

summer

N

winter

N

fall

Read a Diagram

This diagram shows how the seasons change as Earth revolves around the Sun.

Earth's axis stays tilted as it revolves. This tips the North Pole closer to the Sun in June. More sunlight reaches that part of Earth. Daylight lasts longer. Summer begins there.

The North Pole tilts away from the Sun later in the year. The sunlight is less direct. Daylight lasts a shorter time. Winter starts then.

Summer

Winter

✅ Quick Check

8. Use the graphic organizer below to summarize how Earth's axis causes the change in seasons.

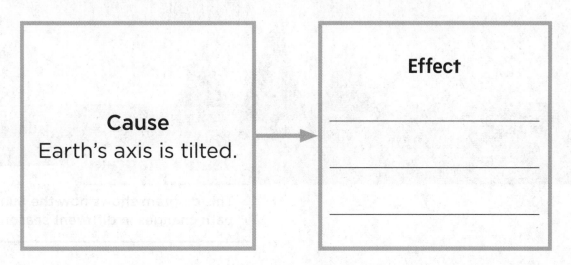

Cause
Earth's axis is tilted.

Effect
_____
_____
_____

How does the Sun's path change from season to season?

The Sun's position in the sky changes during the day. It also changes during the year.

In summer, the northern part of Earth tips toward the Sun. The Sun appears higher in the sky.

In winter, that part of Earth tips away from the Sun. The Sun appears lower in the sky.

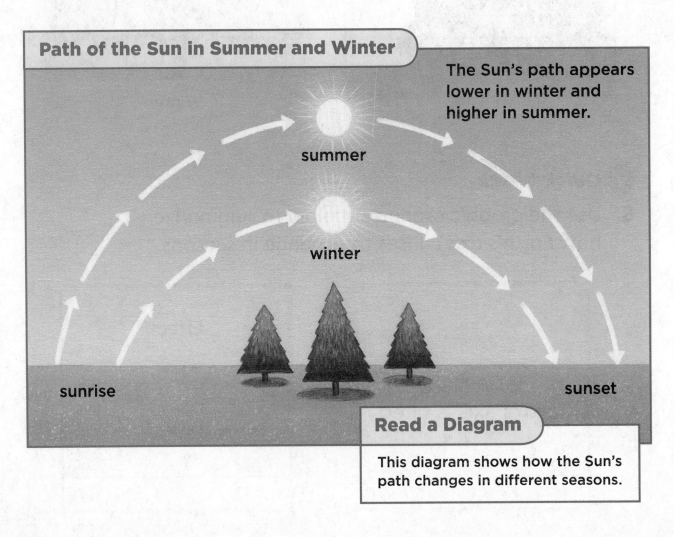

Path of the Sun in Summer and Winter

The Sun's path appears lower in winter and higher in summer.

summer

winter

sunrise

sunset

Read a Diagram

This diagram shows how the Sun's path changes in different seasons.

In spring and fall, the Sun's path is between high and low. Daylight begins to last longer in spring. The air gets warmer. Daylight begins to last less time in fall. The Sun sets sooner each day. The air gets colder.

Summer, 4:00 p.m.

Winter, 4:00 p.m.

▲ Daylight lasts longer and temperatures are higher here in the summer.

✓ **Quick Check**

Circle the correct answers.

9. It is a bright fall day. Tomorrow the sun will appear (higher/lower) in the sky. It will set (sooner/later).

What are the seasons like in other places?

Picture a line around Earth's middle. The northern part of Earth is on top. The southern part is on the bottom.

Places near Earth's middle are warm most of the year. They get about the same amount of sunlight every day.

▲ A drawing of Earth that shows a middle line, a north part, and a south part.

▲ June at Earth's middle line ①

✓ Quick Check

10. What part of Earth has the most warm days each year?

_____

The tilt of Earth's axis causes temperature changes in places to the north and south. Many of these places have different seasons. It is coldest toward the top (North Pole) and bottom (South Pole) of Earth.

▲ June in California ②

▲ June in Argentina ③

✓ Quick Check

Tell whether each statement is true or false.

11. It is cold much of the time at Earth's middle.

_____

12. Earth's north part is closer to the Sun in June

than Earth's south part. _____

LOG ON ℮-**Review** Summaries and quizzes online @ **www.macmillanmh.com**

What are the phases of the moon?

Some nights the Moon is a full circle. On other nights you can only see part of it. The shapes that we see are called the **phases** of the Moon.

The phase of the Moon is the part you can see on a clear night. There are 8 main phases of th Moon.

Phases of the Moon

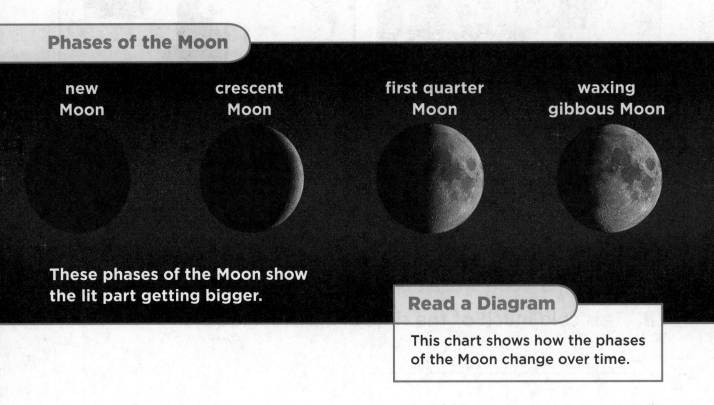

| new Moon | crescent Moon | first quarter Moon | waxing gibbous Moon |

These phases of the Moon show the lit part getting bigger.

Read a Diagram

This chart shows how the phases of the Moon change over time.

Sometimes we see more of the Moon from one night to the next. Other times we see less each night. On some nights you cannot see the Moon at all.

▲ A full Moon rises.

| full Moon | waning gibbous Moon | last quarter Moon | crescent Moon |

These phases of the Moon show the lit part getting smaller.

 **Quick Check**

13. Look at the diagram. Which phase of the Moon cannot be seen at all?

_____

_____

Why does the Moon's shape seem to change?

The Moon is shaped like a ball. It revolves around Earth. This orbit makes its shape appear to change.

Half of the Moon is always lit by the Sun. The other half is in darkness.

The Moon takes about four weeks to finish one orbit. It goes through all of its phases in that time. This is called the **lunar cycle**. The diagram shows how the Moon's shape appears to change over the lunar cycle.

Full Moon

Moon's Orbit

sunlight

third quarter Moon Our view of the Moon from Earth 21 days after the new Moon.

new Moon You cannot see a new Moon.

full Moon Our view of the Moon from Earth 14 days after the new Moon.

first quarter Moon Our view of the Moon from Earth 7 days after the new Moon.

Read a Diagram

This diagram shows how and why the Moon's phases change during the Moon's orbit around Earth.

 Quick Check

14. If there was a new Moon last night, how long will it be until the next full Moon?

_____

What is a lunar eclipse?

Once in a while the Moon may change suddenly in the night sky. It may seem to get darker as you watch. This is called a lunar eclipse.

An eclipse happens when Earth is between the Sun and the Moon. This blocks the Sun's light. It can no longer reach the Moon.

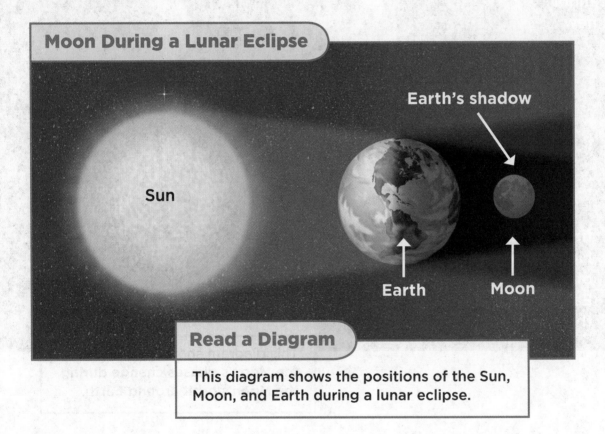

Moon During a Lunar Eclipse

Earth's shadow

Sun

Earth

Moon

Read a Diagram

This diagram shows the positions of the Sun, Moon, and Earth during a lunar eclipse.

✓ Quick Check

15. What blocks the Sun's light during a lunar eclipse?

During an eclipse, darkness covers the face of the Moon. This is Earth's shadow. As the Moon moves, it will leave Earth's shadow. The face of the Moon will be bright again.

▲ During a lunar eclipse, the Moon may turn red.

 Quick Check

16. Use the graphic organizer below to summarize a lunar eclipse.

Before _____

↓

During _____

↓

After _____

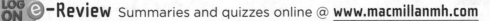

Draw a line between the word and its definition.

1. axis

to spin or turn

2. lunar cycle

the path an object takes as it moves around another object

3. orbit

any shape of the Moon that we see

4. phase

a line through the middle of a spinning thing

5. revolve

to move around another object in a circular path

6. rotate

the time it takes the Moon to go through all its phases

CHAPTER 5

Our Solar System

What objects do we see in the night sky?

Vocabulary

planet A large sphere, or ball, that moves around the Sun.

solar system The Sun, the planets, and other objects.

star A hot, glowing ball of gases.

asteroid A large piece of rock or metal in space.

comet A chunk of ice mixed with rocks and dust moving through space.

meteor A small piece of ice, rock, or metal that has broken off a comet or asteroid.

telescope A tool to make far away objects appear closer and larger.

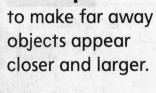

lens A piece of clear material that affects the path of light rays.

constellation A group of stars that forms a picture.

What is the solar system?

The **solar system** is made up of the Sun, the planets, and other objects.

The Sun is a star. A **star** is a hot, glowing ball of gases. The Sun is the closest star to Earth.

✓ Quick Check

I. Why can we see the Sun?

_____

_____

The Solar System

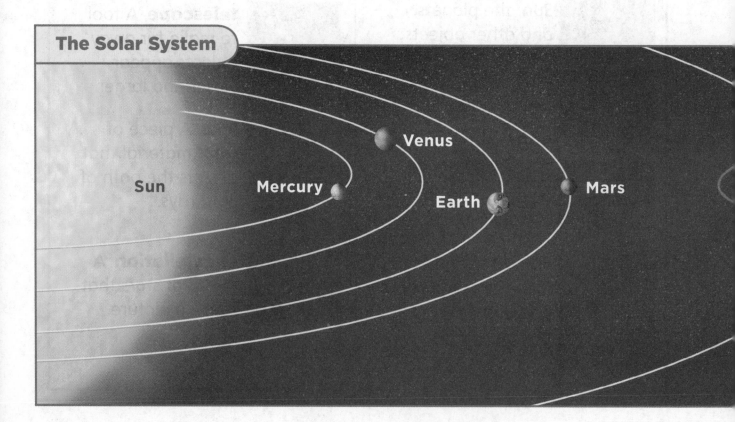

Sun   Mercury   Venus   Earth   Mars

A **planet** is a large sphere, or ball, in space that orbits a star. The planets in our solar system are Mercury, Venus, Earth, Mars, Jupiter, Saturn, Uranus, and Neptune. They travel, or *revolve*, around the Sun.

✓ **Quick Check**

2. What makes up the solar system?

_____

_____

_____

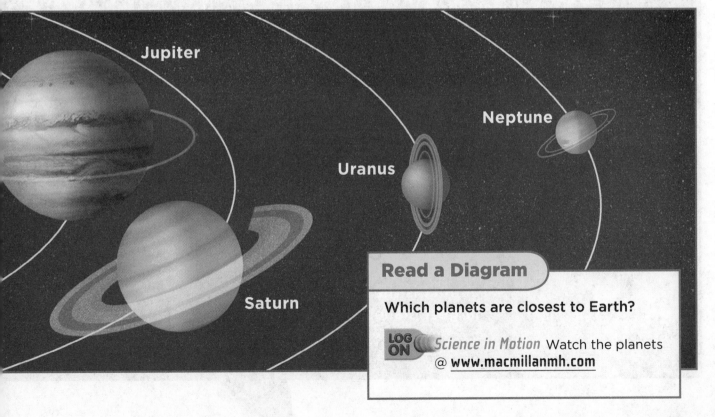

Jupiter

Neptune

Uranus

Saturn

Read a Diagram

Which planets are closest to Earth?

LOG ON *Science in Motion* Watch the planets @ www.macmillanmh.com

What are the planets?

The four planets closest to the Sun are Mercury, Venus, Earth, and Mars. These are the **inner planets**. They are warmer than the other planets because they are closer to the Sun.

The four planets farthest from the Sun are Jupiter, Saturn, Uranus, and Neptune. They are the **outer planets**. Jupiter, Saturn, Uranus, and Neptune are the largest planets in the solar system.

Inner Planets

◄ **Mercury** is the planet closest to the Sun.

◄ **Venus** is the hottest planet.

Outer Planets

Saturn has thousands of beautiful rings. ▶

◄ **Jupiter** is the largest planet.

The solar system also has some dwarf planets. Pluto is now called a dwarf planet.

✔ Quick Check

3. Why are Mercury, Venus, Earth, and Mars the warmest planets?

_____

_____

_____

◀ Earth is the only planet with oxygen, liquid water, and living things.

◀ Mars is called the Red Planet because it has reddish-brown soil.

◀ Uranus is called the "sideways" planet because it turns on its side.

◀ Neptune is more than two billion miles from Earth.

What else is in our solar system?

Asteroids (AS•tuh•roydz), comets
(KAH•muhts), and meteors (MEE•tee•uhrz)
also orbit the Sun. **Asteroids** are large pieces
of rock or metal. They may be pieces of a
broken planet.

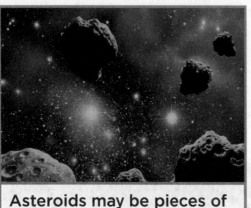

Asteroids may be pieces of
planets that broke apart.

Comets are chunks of ice mixed with rocks
and dust moving through space.

A comet may have
a glowing tail.

Meteors are small pieces of ice, rock, or metal that have broken off a comet or asteroid. A meteor that hits Earth is called a *meteorite*.

Most meteorites are small. ▶

This crater was made when a huge meteorite crashed into Earth thousands of years ago.

✔ *Quick Check*

4. How does a meteor form?

_____

_____

_____

 e-Review Summaries and quizzes online @ **www.macmillanmh.com**

What is a telescope?

Objects in space are far away. A **telescope** is a tool that helps us see them. It makes far objects appear bigger and nearer.

Telescopes take in light with a **lens**. This piece of clear material can change the path of light. This helps us see distant things in more detail.

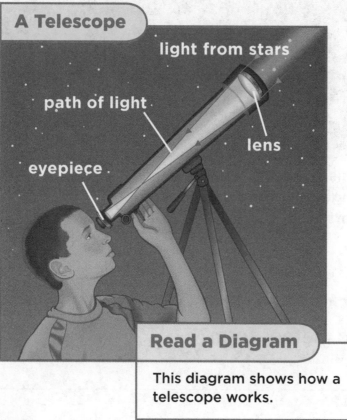

A Telescope

light from stars

path of light

lens

eyepiece

Read a Diagram

This diagram shows how a telescope works.

✓ *Quick Check*

Circle the correct answer.

5. Why would a scientist use a telescope to look at the Moon?

Telescopes on Earth do a good job. Telescopes sent into space are even better. The Hubble Space Telescope travels high above our planet. It takes pictures to send back to scientists on Earth.

Other kinds of telescopes can help scientists see into space. Radio telescopes take in radio waves. Then a computer turns the data into pictures.

Hubble Space Telescope

radio telescopes

How did we learn about space?

People long ago thought Earth was the center of the solar system. They thought the Sun traveled around Earth.

Copernicus was a scientist. In 1543 he said that the Sun was the center of the solar system. Galileo was another scientist. In 1609 he used a telescope to show that Copernicus was right.

▲ Galileo helped us learn about the solar system.

 Quick Check

6. What did Galileo learn about Earth with his telescope?

_____

Telescopes helped us learn even more about space. Scientists found other planets, such as Uranus and Neptune. Telescopes let us see more than we can with our eyes. We now know that there are billions of objects in space.

Galileo used this telescope to learn about objects in our solar system. ▶

✔ Quick Check

Circle the letter of the correct answer to the question.

7. What did people believe about the solar system before Copernicus?

   a. that the Sun revolved around Earth

   b. that Earth revolved around the Moon

   c. that Earth revolved around the Sun

   d. that the Sun revolved around the Moon

LOG ON **e-Review** Summaries and quizzes online @ **www.macmillanmh.com**

What are stars?

Stars are hot, glowing balls of gases. Some stars group together. Our solar system is in a group of stars called the Milky Way.

Stars of all sizes look like tiny points of light in the night sky. They are very far away. The Sun is the closest star to Earth. Its light makes it too bright to see the other stars during the daytime.

Stars fill the night sky.

Stars do not move. However, they appear to move across the night sky. They all seem to go in the same direction. This is because the Earth rotates, or spins.

Some objects in the night sky are moving. These "stars" are really planets. They may change position as they move around the Sun.

Saturn
Mars

Venus

Mercury

Stars and planets look alike in the night sky.

This photo taken by the Hubble Space Telescope shows a very large star.

 **Quick Check**

8. Why do stars appear to move across the night sky?

What is a constellation?

A **constellation** is a group of stars. The group forms a kind of picture. Some even have stories about them. People used constellations to make sense of the night sky. Scientists still use them today.

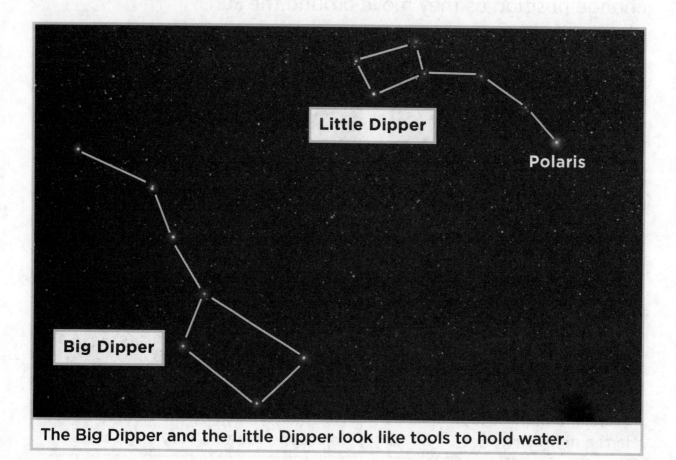

Little Dipper

Polaris

Big Dipper

The Big Dipper and the Little Dipper look like tools to hold water.

✔ Quick Check

Tell whether each statement is true or false.

9. People today no longer use constellations. _____

10. People told stories about some of the constellations.

_____

Constellations seem to move as Earth rotates and revolves. People long ago studied these changes. They used them to tell time. Farmers used them to tell the seasons. Sailors could tell direction by the positions of stars.

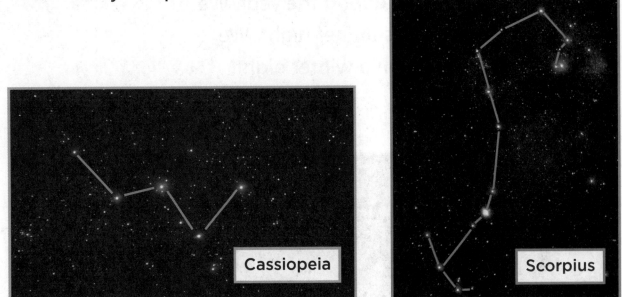

Cassiopeia

Scorpius

✅ Quick Check

11. Use the graphic organizer below to list three ways that constellations helped people.

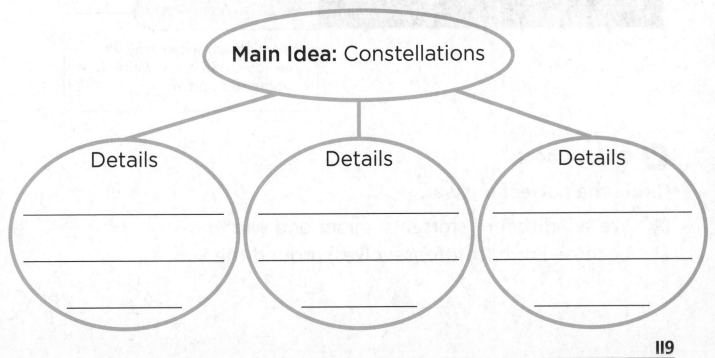

Main Idea: Constellations

Details

Details

Details

Why do we see different stars during different seasons?

The night sky looks different from one season to the next. This is because Earth revolves around the Sun during the year. We face one direction on a summer night. We face another direction on a winter night.

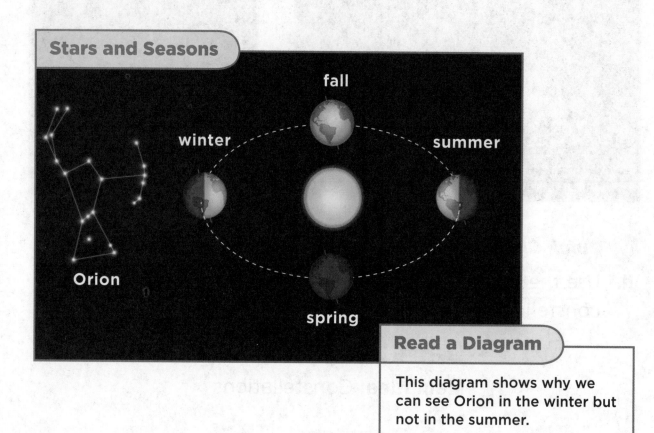

Stars and Seasons

fall

winter

summer

Orion

spring

Read a Diagram

This diagram shows why we can see Orion in the winter but not in the summer.

✓ *Quick Check*

Circle the correct answer.

12. We see different stars in summer and winter because Earth (rotates/revolves) around the Sun.

We can see Orion in the winter. We look out in its direction at night.

We cannot see Orion in the summer. It is in the same direction as the Sun. We look out in the opposite direction at night. Different stars and constellations fill the night sky.

We can see these stars in Orion only on winter nights.

✅ Quick Check

13. We face Orion during the day in summer. Why is it

not visible? _____

_____

Our Solar System

a. planet	c. solar system	e. star	g. asteroid	i. comet
b. meteor	d. constellation	f. lens	h. telescope	

Match the correct letter with the description.

1. _____ A small piece of ice, rock, or metal that has broken off a comet or asteroid.

2. _____ The Sun, the planets, and other objects.

3. _____ A group of stars that forms a picture.

4. _____ A chunk of ice mixed with rocks and dust moving though space.

5. _____ A hot, glowing ball of gases in space.

6. _____ A tool to make far away objects appear closer and larger.

7. _____ A large piece of rock or metal in space.

8. _____ A piece of clear material that affects the path of light rays.

9. _____ A large sphere, or ball, in space that moves around a star.

Our Solar System

Find the words from the box in the word search.
Words can run up, down, and across.

planet	solar system	comet	asteroid
meteor	constellation	lens	telescope
star			

```
P S O L A R S Y S T E M O
T E L I D K T X Q C T E D
E N R V T Y A O I E M T A
L E N S C P R L R L U E S
E R A F N T K Z Q N F O T
S Z R D Y C O M E T P R E
C G I X H I B A N K S U R
O T W I N F T R U A C D O
P B O P L A N E T L R H I
E K R V B I O C B G E Z D
R S L M N F G I S C P V L
C O N S T E L L A T I O N
```

CHAPTER 6

Matter

Vocabulary

matter anything that takes up space

mass a measure of how much matter is in an object

solid matter in a state that has a definite shape and volume

liquid matter in a state that has a definite volume but no definite shape

gas matter in a state that has no definite shape or volume

melt to change from a solid to a liquid

evaporate to change slowly from liquid to gas

The Big Idea

What are some forms of matter and how can they change?

 **freeze** to change from liquid to solid

 **condense** to change from gas to liquid

 **element** a basic building block of matter

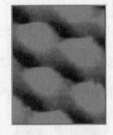 **atom** the smallest part of an element that has the properties of that element

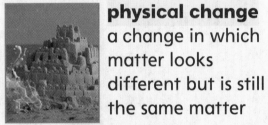 **physical change** a change in which matter looks different but is still the same matter

 **chemical change** a change that causes a new kind of matter to form

What is matter?

The things around you have different shapes, sizes, colors, and smells. They are all alike in one way. They are all kinds of **matter**.

Matter is anything that takes up space. A thing's **mass** tells you how much matter it has. A pan balance like this one can measure mass.

bag of popcorn

bag of marbles

The marbles have more mass than the popcorn.

✔ Quick Check

I. How can you measure the amount of matter in a thing?

Each kind of matter has properties. These help you describe matter. Some common properties are:

taste   shape

color   smell

size   feel

mass   sound

You can observe and measure the properties of matter. They help you sort different kinds of matter.

▲ Matter can have many shapes, sizes, and colors.

How do we classify matter?

Matter can take three states:

solid

liquid

gas

A **solid** takes up a certain amount of space. It also keeps its shape. Most of the things you see are solids.

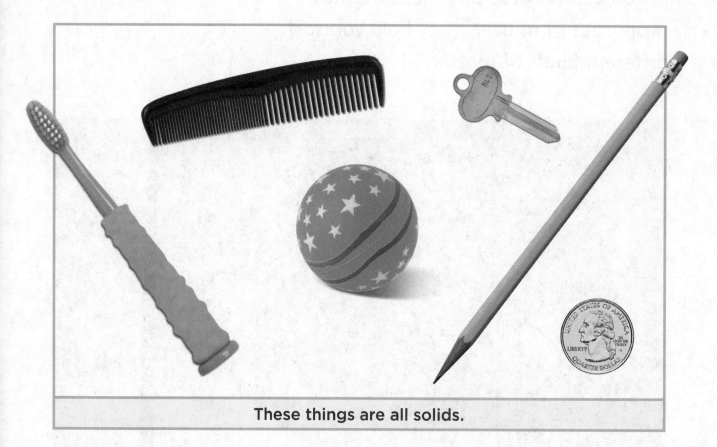

These things are all solids.

✓ Quick Check

Circle the correct answer to the question.

2. Which of the following is a state of matter?

color   mass   liquid   size

A **liquid** also takes up a certain amount of space. However, it does not keep its shape. A liquid takes the shape of the thing that holds it.

A **gas**, like a liquid, does not keep its shape.

Unlike a liquid, a gas spreads out to fill different amounts of space.

Each container has 100 mL of liquid inside.

◀ You cannot see most gases, but you know a gas is inside these balloons because it gives them their shape.

What happens when heat is added to matter?

Matter gains energy when it is heated. This can change its state.

If a solid is heated enough, it will **melt**. This means the solid turns into a liquid. Ice is water in its solid state. It does not take much heat to melt it. Rocks can also melt. It takes a lot of heat to melt them.

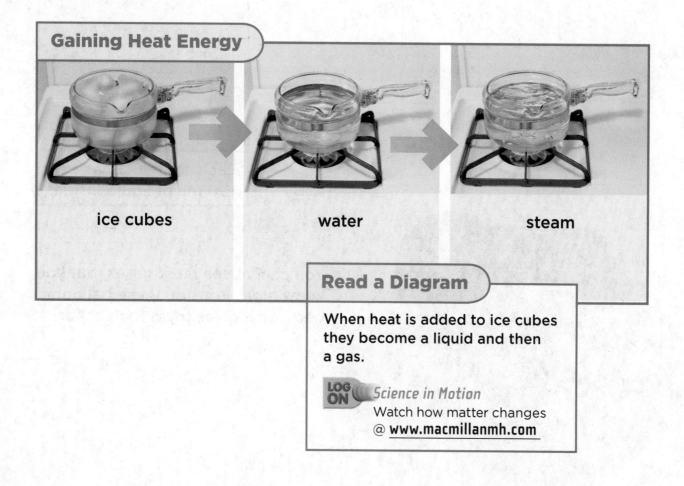

Gaining Heat Energy

ice cubes   water   steam

Read a Diagram

When heat is added to ice cubes they become a liquid and then a gas.

LOG ON *Science in Motion*
Watch how matter changes
@ www.macmillanmh.com

If a liquid is heated enough, it will **evaporate**. This means it turns into a gas. This invisible gas is called water vapor. The Sun can heat water too. The water will turn into gas and go into the air.

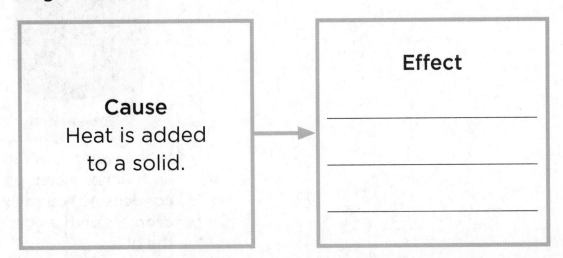

▲ The water in these wet clothes will evaporate in the Sun. Then the clothes will be dry.

 Quick Check

3. Use the graphic organizer below to show how heat can change matter.

Cause	Effect
Heat is added to a solid.	_____ _____ _____

What happens when matter loses energy?

Matter gains energy from heat. Matter can also lose energy. If matter loses enough heat, it may change its state.

A liquid will **freeze** if it loses enough heat energy. This means the liquid changes to a solid.

A gas will **condense** if it loses enough heat energy. This means that the gas changes to a liquid.

▲ Juice freezes to become a solid that you can eat.

✅ *Quick Check*

Fill in the blanks.

4. When matter freezes, it turns

   from a _____

   into a _____.

▲ When water vapor in the air touches a cold glass, it condenses. You see water droplets on the outside of the glass.

On a cool morning, small droplets of water may form on grass and other objects. These water droplets are called *dew*. Dew forms when water vapor in the air touches a cool object. The water vapor loses heat energy and condenses to form liquid water.

▲ Dew formed on this spider web when water vapor cooled and condensed.

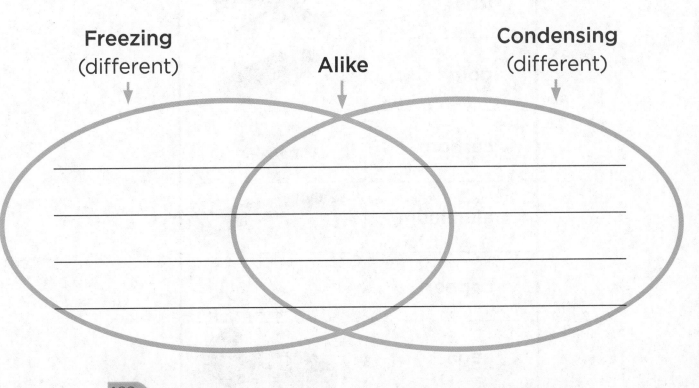

✔ Quick Check

Fill in the diagram to show how freezing and condensing are alike and different.

Freezing
(different)

Alike

Condensing
(different)

LOG ON **e-Review** Summaries and quizzes online @ www.macmillanmh.com

What are elements?

All matter is made up of **elements**. An element is a building block of matter.

People long ago thought there were four elements. These were earth, wind, fire, and water.

We now know that these were not real elements. Tools have helped us observe over 100 elements. Some are listed below.

Elements	
iron	
gold	
carbon	
aluminum	
copper	
neon	

Most matter is made up of more than one element. Water is made up of two elements, oxygen and hydrogen. Sugar contains those two elements plus carbon.

Elements join together in many ways. They help build all the matter in our world.

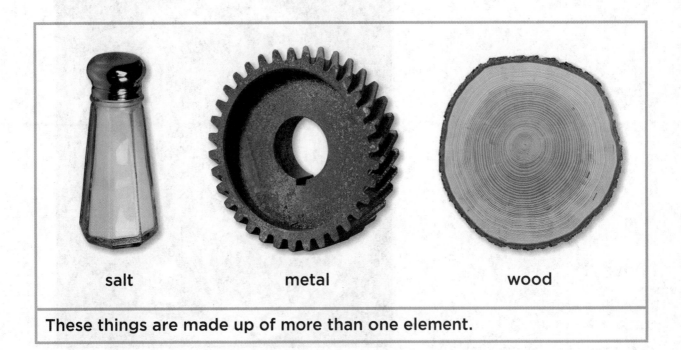

salt   metal   wood

These things are made up of more than one element.

✔ Quick Check

Circle the correct answers.

5. Which of the following is an element?

   fire   gold   water   color

6. Which of the following is made up of more than one element?

   fire   gold   water   color

What are atoms?

Elements are made up of tiny parts called atoms. An **atom** is the smallest part of an element that still has the properties of that element. All atoms of an element are the same.

Atoms are very small. Compare the size of an apple with the size of Earth. The difference between an atom and an apple is about the same.

✔ Quick Check

Fill in the blanks.

7. How would two atoms from the same element compare

with one another? _____

_____

Atoms are too small to see with our eyes. Scientists must use tools to observe them. A microscope is one of these tools. A powerful microscope can make atoms appear much larger.

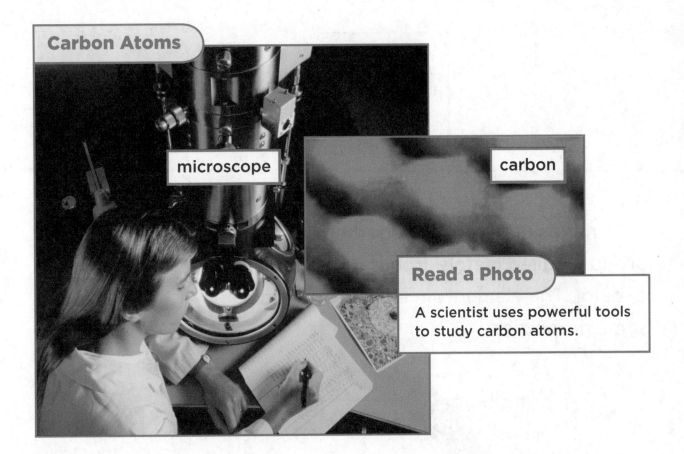

Carbon Atoms

microscope

carbon

Read a Photo

A scientist uses powerful tools to study carbon atoms.

✔️ *Quick Check*

8. Salt is made up of the elements sodium and chlorine. A scientist can use a microscope to look at salt. What kinds of

atoms would she see? _____

_____

How do we arrange elements?

Scientists use a table to arrange the elements. You can see it on the next page.

Each element has a symbol. For example, sodium has the symbol Na.

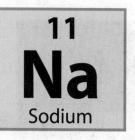

11
Na
Sodium

Elements are grouped together. One group is called metals. Iron is an example of a metal. The elements in each group share some properties.

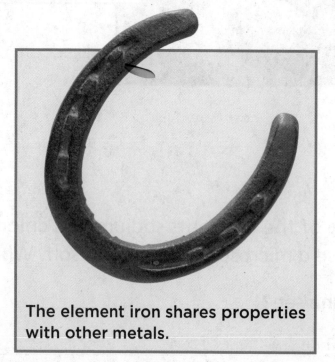

The element iron shares properties with other metals.

The Elements

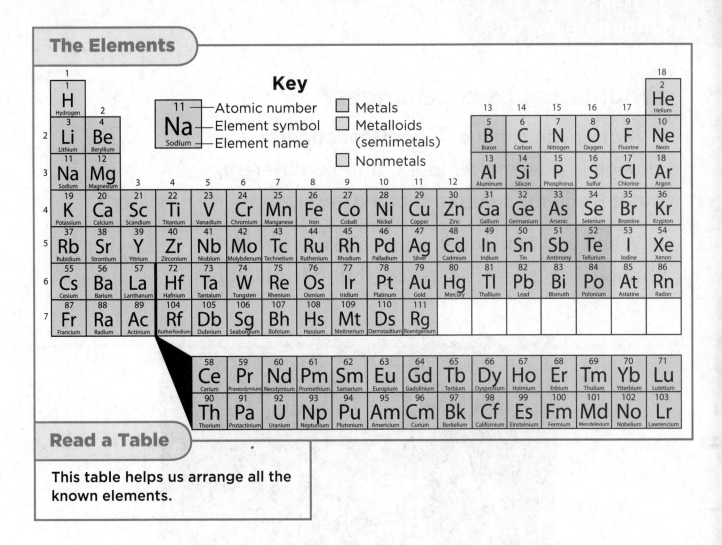

Key

11 ← Atomic number
Na ← Element symbol
Sodium ← Element name

☐ Metals
☐ Metalloids (semimetals)
☐ Nonmetals

Read a Table

This table helps us arrange all the known elements.

Quick Check

Use the table to tell whether each statement is true or false.

9. The element titanium is a metal. _____

10. The symbol for carbon is Ca. _____

11. Nonmetals are grouped on the left side of the table.

_____

LOG ON e-Review Summaries and quizzes online @ www.macmillanmh.com

What are physical changes?

Matter can change. A **physical change** is a change in how matter looks. It looks different, but it is still the same kind of matter.

When you tear paper, you make a physical change. The paper is in pieces, but it is still paper.

This sand was shaped to look like a castle, but it is still sand.

✅ **Quick Check**

12. Explain why making a ball from a piece of clay is a physical change. _____

_____

Matter can change its state. This is also a physical change. Liquid water may freeze into ice. It is still water. The same elements make up water in all of its states. It is still the same kind of matter.

You can put different kinds of matter together. The kinds of matter may not change. A salad is an example.

▲ A liquid may freeze. This is a physical change.

What are chemical changes?

Some changes cause matter to turn into other kinds of matter. This is a **chemical change**. The properties of the new matter are different.

A burning log goes through a chemical change. The log starts as wood. Fire turns it to ash. Some gas also forms. These kinds of matter are different from wood. They have different properties.

▲ A chemical change turns wood into ash and gas.

Chemical changes also take place in food. Food may spoil as it gets old. It may change color. It may smell or taste bad.

Baking also causes a chemical change. The new food may taste different from the things used to make it. It may even be a new color.

A Chemical Change

ingredients

dough

bread

Read a Photo

Baking caused the bread dough to undergo a chemical change.

✅ *Quick Check*

13. Why is baking a cake an example of a chemical change?

What are the signs of a chemical change?

Most times you can tell when a chemical change happens. Here are some signs to look for:

light and heat
color change
gas formation

A burning candle gives off light and heat. A chemical change is taking place.

✓ *Quick Check*

Circle the correct answer.

14. Which of the following is a chemical change?

ice melts   glass breaks   paper burns

Iron can turn to rust if it is left outside in the rain.

When the iron in this truck rusts, it changes color. This shows that a chemical change is taking place. ▶

Gas may form when two kinds of matter mix.

A gas was formed by the chemical change that happened when two kinds of matter were mixed. ▶

Matter

Use each word once to fill in the blanks.

solid	matter	evaporates	liquid
melts	mass	gas	

1. When a _____ freezes, it turns into ice.

2. _____ tells us how much matter is in an object.

3. _____ is anything that takes up space.

4. When ice _____ it changes from a(n)

   _____ to a liquid.

5. When a liquid _____ it changes into a(n)

   _____ .

CHAPTER 7

Energy

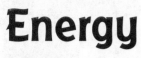 **What are some forms of energy and how can they change?**

Vocabulary

energy the ability to do work

potential energy energy that is stored inside matter

kinetic energy energy in the form of movement or motion

fuel a source of stored energy

wave a change that moves through matter or space

What is energy?

Energy is the ability to do work. Energy can make matter move, grow, or change.

Energy can make things move. A soccer player uses energy to kick a ball. Energy moves from the player's foot to the ball. This energy makes the ball move to a new place.

These penguins need energy to move.

Energy can also make things change. Energy in the air can cause a physical change in ice. It can turn it from a solid to a liquid. Energy from fire can burn wood. This chemical change turns wood into smoke, ash, and gas.

Energy can also make things grow. Energy helps plants make food and grow. All living things need energy to survive.

◄ When someone kicks a ball, energy makes it move.

✔ Quick Check

I. Summarize three things that energy can do to matter.

1. _____

2. _____

3. _____

What are some forms of energy?

There are many forms of energy. Some are listed below.

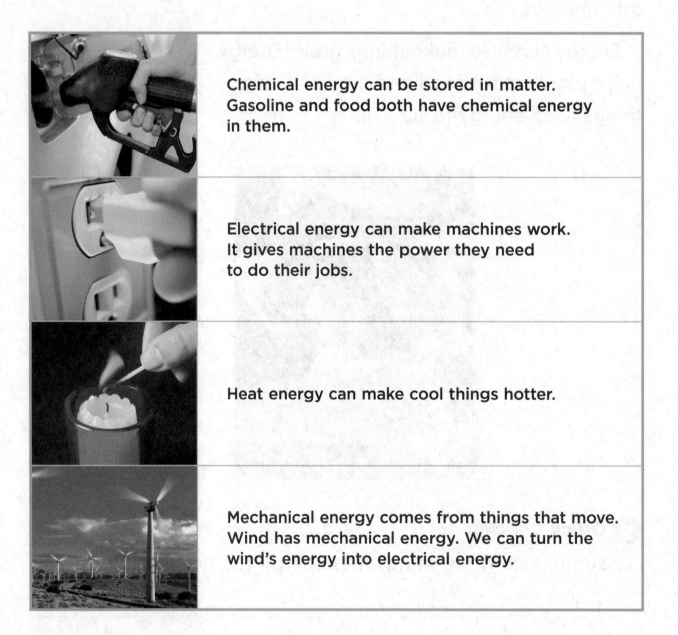

Chemical energy can be stored in matter. Gasoline and food both have chemical energy in them.

Electrical energy can make machines work. It gives machines the power they need to do their jobs.

Heat energy can make cool things hotter.

Mechanical energy comes from things that move. Wind has mechanical energy. We can turn the wind's energy into electrical energy.

▲ Friction causes mechanical energy from your moving hands to change into heat energy. This makes your hands feel warmer.

 Quick Check

2. What kind of energy comes from each example?

an apple _____

a burning candle _____

a moving car _____

What is Earth's main source of energy?

The Sun is Earth's main source of energy. The energy comes to Earth in the form of light. Light is a form of energy. Some parts of Earth get more light than others. This is because Earth has a tilted axis.

▲ The Sun is the main source of energy for living things.

 **Quick Check**

3. How does the Sun's energy reach Earth? _____

_____

▲ When she eats these grapes, some of the Sun's energy will be inside her.

The Sun's energy helps plants make food to live. Some energy from the Sun stays in the plants.

The Sun heats up some places more than others. Air moves from cooler places to warmer places. This causes wind. We can use the wind's energy. It can make a windmill turn. A turning windmill can be used to make electrical energy.

✓ Quick Check

4. The Sun's energy can cause wind. What form of energy has

   it changed into? _____

   _____

How does the Sun's energy change matter?

The Sun's energy can add heat to matter. This can melt solids into liquids. It can make liquids evaporate.

▲ The Sun's rays can heat and melt the snowman.

✓ Quick Check

5. What causes ice to melt on a sunny day? _____

_____

The Sun can change snow and ice into liquid. It can turn water into vapor. Clouds are made of this vapor.

Vapor in the air cools. It changes back into a liquid. It may then fall back to Earth as rain or snow.

This happens over and over. The same water evaporates into the air. Then it falls back down. The Sun makes all this happen.

Energy from the Sun causes Earth's weather.

LOG ON e-Review Summaries and quizzes online @ www.macmillanmh.com

What is potential energy and kinetic energy?

A toy car at rest needs energy to move. You can move it to the top of a hill. This gives it more energy.

That energy may not be used right away. If the car is at rest, the energy is stored. Stored energy is also called **potential energy**.

You can put the toy car on the hill and let go. It will move down the hill. It uses its stored energy to move. When a thing moves, it has **kinetic energy**.

This toy car has potential energy at the top of the hill. ▶

A roller coaster at the top of the track has stored energy. It has more energy if the track is very high. Then it races down the track. It has kinetic energy as it moves.

◀ A moving roller coaster changes potential energy into kinetic energy.

✓ **Quick Check**

Circle the correct answer.

6. Which has *less* stored energy?

a car at the top of a hill

a car at the bottom of a hill

What are some sources of stored energy?

Fuel is something with stored chemical energy. Wood, gas, batteries, and food are examples. We can change the form of the energy in these things.

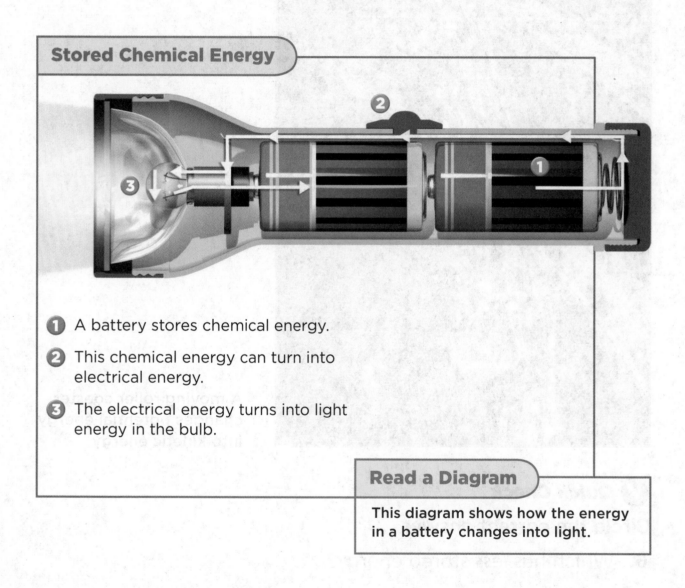

Stored Chemical Energy

1. A battery stores chemical energy.

2. This chemical energy can turn into electrical energy.

3. The electrical energy turns into light energy in the bulb.

Read a Diagram

This diagram shows how the energy in a battery changes into light.

We burn wood for light and heat energy. We burn gas to make cars move. We eat food to help us move and grow. Our bodies turn the food into other forms of energy.

An apple gives this boy energy for the game.

✓ Quick Check

7. Why would you be hungry after doing hard work? _____

_____

_____

How is stored energy changed?

Many machines change stored energy into kinetic energy. A stove can turn gas into heat.

A watch may have a spring inside. The spring gets potential energy when you wind the watch. This energy makes the hands on the watch move.

◀ The stored energy in rocket fuel can send the space shuttle into space.

Cars use the stored energy in gasoline. They turn it into mechanical energy. This makes the car move.

Some energy turns into heat. When you move, you are using stored energy from food. This makes you feel warmer. Your body might sweat to stay cool.

▲ Playing sports uses energy and makes you warmer.

✔ *Quick Check*

Circle the best answer for each question.

8. A stove can turn fuel into _____ energy.

mechanical   gas   heat   chemical

9. A watch uses a spring to make _____ energy.

mechanical   light   heat   electrical

LOG ON e-**Review** Summaries and quizzes online @ **www.macmillanmh.com**

How can energy move through objects?

Energy can move from one thing to another. You can push a bowling ball forward. Energy moves from your arm to your hand to the ball. The ball may roll and hit some pins. The pins may fall down. Energy moves from the ball to the pins.

Energy moves from the ball to the pins.

 **Quick Check**

Tell whether the statement is true or false.

10. An object cannot give its energy to another object.

_____

One moving thing can make another thing move. The energy goes from one to the other.

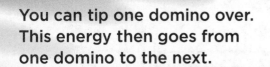

You can tip one domino over. This energy then goes from one domino to the next.

 Quick Check

11. Show how energy moves from one thing to another in bowling. Use the graphic organizer below.

↓

↓

↓

How is energy transferred by waves?

Some energy moves in waves. A **wave** is a change that moves through matter or space. Sound and light energy move in waves.

Ocean waves carry energy. This energy can move to things in the water. The energy can move things up and down.

Energy in Waves

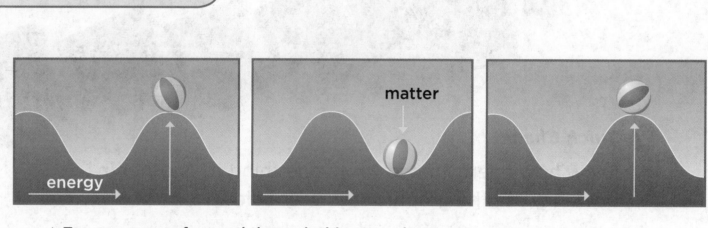

matter

energy

▲ Energy moves forward through this wave, but the ball moves up and down.

Read a Diagram

This diagram shows how energy in a wave makes a ball move up and down.

Waves move in different ways. Ocean waves move in one way. They go up and down.

Energy in the water moves forward. Objects in the water move up and down. They do not move forward. The energy does move forward.

Wave energy lifts this surfer up. His own energy helps him move forward.

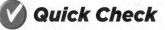 **Quick Check**

12. A stick floats in deep water. A wave passes. How does the stick's position change? _____

_____

This boy makes the guitar strings move. Then the strings make sound.

How does sound energy move?

Sound also moves in waves. These waves do not move up and down. They move back and forth.

Sound is a kind of mechanical energy. Something must move to make sound. You move a guitar string to make sound.

1 Sound waves move through the air. Some of them enter your ear.

2 Your ear has many small parts. Different sound waves make them move in different ways.

3 This lets you hear different things. Your ear tells your brain about the sounds.

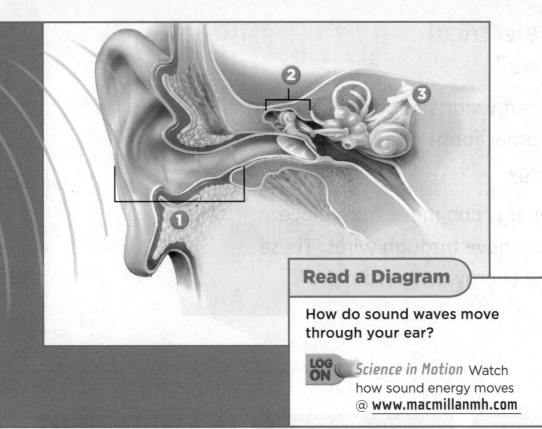

Read a Diagram

How do sound waves move through your ear?

LOG ON *Science in Motion* Watch how sound energy moves @ **www.macmillanmh.com**

✓ *Quick Check*

13. How does the movement of sound waves differ from

ocean waves? _____

_____

14. How does your ear let you hear sound?

_____

_____

 e-Review Summaries and quizzes online @ **www.macmillanmh.com**

How does electrical energy move?

Electrical energy starts in power plants. They change other forms of energy into electrical energy.

Electrical energy can move from place to place. It can move through wires. These wires carry the energy away from the power plant.

| power plant | electrical wires | house wires |

Wires bring electrical energy into your home. Outlets in your home connect to the wires.

You can plug a machine into these outlets. Machines then change the form of the energy. Some can move. Others can make light, heat, or sound.

outlet

 Quick Check

15. How does electrical energy get from a power plant to your home?

First _____

Next _____

Last _____

e-Review Summaries and quizzes online @ **www.macmillanmh.com**

Draw a line between each word and its definition. Use each word only once to complete the sentences.

1. energy

2. potential energy

3. kinetic energy

4. fuel

5. wave

a change that moves through matter or space

energy in the form of movement or motion

the ability to do work

a source of stored energy

energy that is stored inside matter

6. A car speeding around a track is an example of

_____.

7. Sound is a type of energy that moves in a(n) _____.

8. Gasoline and firewood are both examples of _____.

9. When you pick up an object, you use _____.

10. The power inside a battery is an example of

_____.

CHAPTER 8

Light

The Big Idea What is light and how does it travel?

Vocabulary

light a form of energy made of waves that move up and down

shadow the dark area that results when light is blocked

reflection light that bounces off an object

transparent able to let all light pass through

absorb to take in

translucent able to let some but not all light pass through

opaque not able to let light pass through

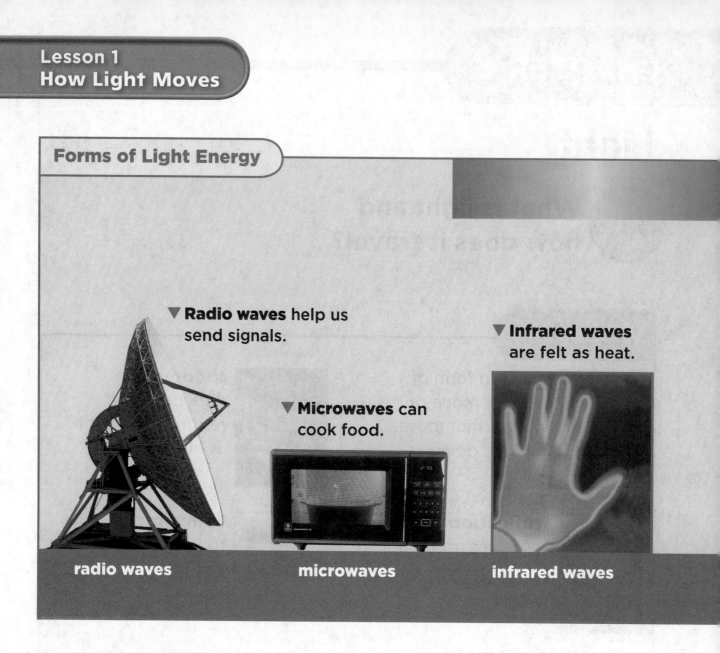

Forms of Light Energy

▼ **Radio waves** help us send signals.

▼ **Microwaves** can cook food.

▼ **Infrared waves** are felt as heat.

radio waves   microwaves   infrared waves

What is light?

Light is a form of energy. It is made of waves that move up and down.

You can see some light waves. We call these waves visible light. You can see all the colors of the rainbow.

You cannot see the other kinds of light waves. They help us in other ways. Doctors use X-rays to check your bones. Microwaves help us heat our food.

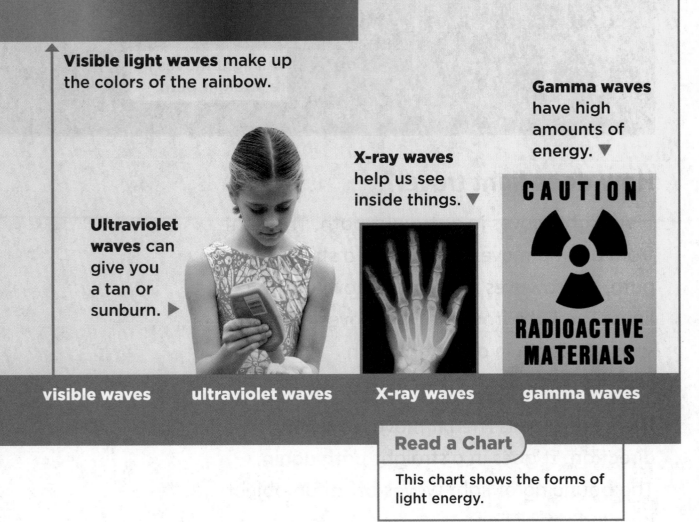

Visible light waves make up the colors of the rainbow.

Gamma waves have high amounts of energy. ▼

X-ray waves help us see inside things. ▼

Ultraviolet waves can give you a tan or sunburn. ▶

CAUTION

RADIOACTIVE MATERIALS

visible waves   ultraviolet waves   X-ray waves   gamma waves

Read a Chart

This chart shows the forms of light energy.

✔ *Quick Check*

Circle the correct answer

I. Which kind of light wave can you see with your eyes?

infrared   visible   radio   ultraviolet

All light moves in a straight path.

How does light travel?

All light moves in a straight path. The light from a lamp moves outward in a straight path. Microwaves in an oven move in straight lines. The light from the Sun moves through space to Earth in a straight path.

Light can hit objects. It may bounce off them like a ball. Then it moves in a new direction. It goes in a straight path again. The bouncing of light waves off of an object is called **reflection**.

Smooth, shiny surfaces reflect a lot of light. A mirror is an example.

✓ *Quick Check*

2. How are microwaves and the Sun's light alike?

A mirror shows us a
reflection of light.

✅ *Quick Check*

3. How is light like a tennis ball? _____

_____

What happens when light hits a rough surface?

A smooth surface makes light bounce back in one direction. The reflection shows us a clear image. A still lake is an example. The water acts like a mirror. We see a clear reflected image.

Smooth water shows a clear reflected image.

✓ Quick Check

4. Predict what will happen to the reflection if wind makes the surface of the lake rough. _____

_____

A rough surface makes light bounce off in many directions. It does not reflect a clear image. What you see may look blurry or foggy.

Light bounces off rough water in many directions.

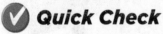 **Quick Check**

Circle the letter of the correct answer.

5. What happens to light as it hits rough water?

   a. It bounces off in the same direction.

   b. It bounces off on many curved paths.

   c. It bounces off in different directions.

   d. It bounces off in a circular path.

How do you see?

Light reflects off objects and goes into your eye. You then see an image of the object.

Some parts of your eye can open and close. They can open to let in more light. This helps you see when it is dark. They can close to let in less light. This helps you see when it is very bright.

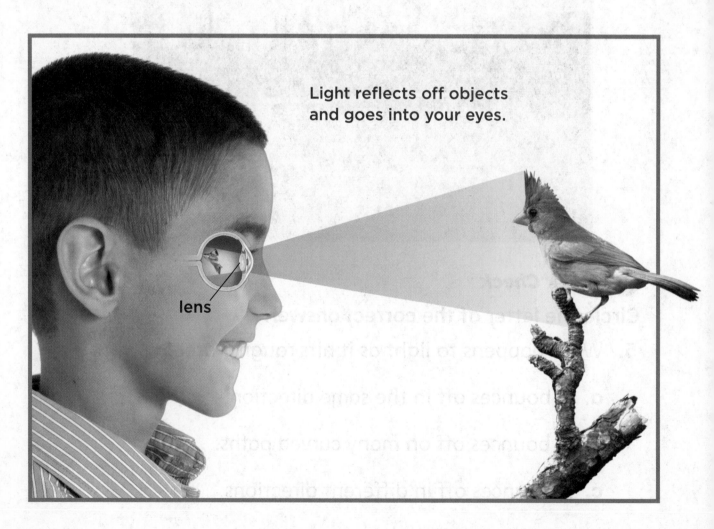

Light reflects off objects and goes into your eyes.

lens

Another part of the eye helps you see things more clearly. This part is called the lens. It helps to send a sharp image to the brain. Your brain can then tell what you are looking at.

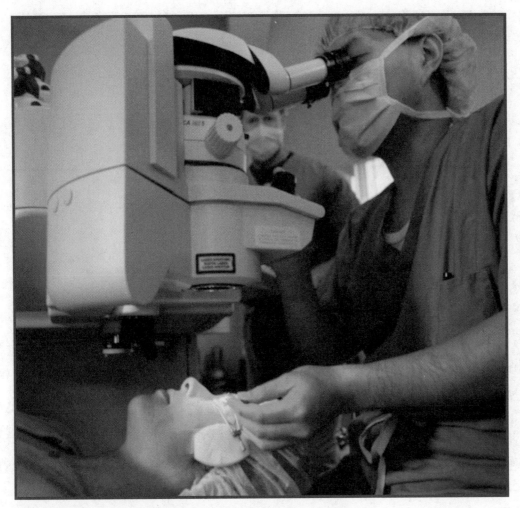

▲ Machines like this microscope can help your eyes see even more.

 **Quick Check**

6. What do parts of your eye do when it gets dark? _____

_____

Why can you see colors?

White light is really made up of seven colors. You can see them in a rainbow. Drops of water can split white light into these colors. So can some kinds of glass.

▲ Raindrops can split sunlight and make a rainbow.

✓ Quick Check

Circle the correct answer.

7. How many colors can you see in a rainbow?

3   5   7   10

Many objects **absorb**, or take in, some of
light's colors. Other colors reflect off of them.
We see the colors that reflect off the object.
We do not see colors that the object absorbs.

A green leaf reflects the color green.
It absorbs the other colors in white light.
Our eyes only see the color green.

A red flower reflects the color red.
It absorbs all the other colors.

Seeing Colors

The flower
looks red.

Read a Diagram

The flower absorbs all colors except red.

LOG ON *Science in Motion* Learn about seeing
colors @ **www.macmillanmh.com**

✔ *Quick Check*

8. A green leaf reflects the color _____.

   Our eyes see the color _____.

Why do objects appear black or white?

A black object absorbs all the colors of light. It reflects none of the colors.

A white objects reflects all the colors of light. It absorbs none of the colors.

▲ White patches on this ball reflect more light than black patches.

A filter lets only some colors of light through. It absorbs the rest. For example, white light that passes through a red filter will look red.

If red light hits a white object, only red light can reflect. The object will look red to us. An object's color may look different in different kinds of light.

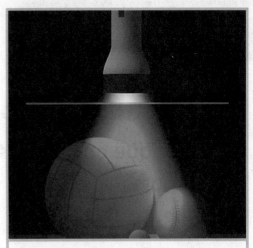

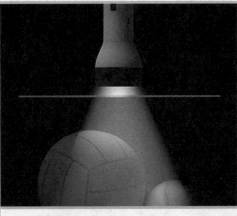

Red light on a white object makes it look red.

Blue light on a white object makes it look blue.

✓ Quick Check

Circle the letter of the correct answer.

9. Which of the following best summarizes how black objects and white objects compare?

    a. Both reflect all the colors of light.

    b. Both absorb all the colors of light.

    c. Black objects reflect all colors and white absorbs them.

    d. White objects reflect all colors and black absorbs them.

LOG ON **e-Review** Summaries and quizzes online @ www.macmillanmh.com

How are shadows formed?

An **opaque** object does not let light energy pass through it. It reflects some light energy as well.

A **shadow** forms when some light energy is blocked. The dark space shows where light has been blocked.

◄ This girl's umbrella blocks light and casts a shadow.

▲ Our bodies are opaque and cast shadows.

All opaque objects block light. They cast shadows. These shadows form away from the source of light. If you face a sunny window, your shadow falls behind you.

You cannot see things behind an opaque object. The object blocks light from reaching your eyes. A brick wall is an example of this. Light from the other side cannot reach you.

✔ **Quick Check**

10. How might you tell if an object is opaque? _____

_____

What affects the shape and size of shadows?

A shadow takes the shape of the object that blocks light. If you stand in the Sun, your shadow takes the shape of your body. Objects with different shapes form shadows with different shapes.

▲ Our shadows show the shapes of our bodies.

Shadows can change size in different kinds of light. Light from above makes a shorter shadow. Light from the side makes a longer shadow.

We can use shadows to tell the time of day. They can tell us where the Sun is in the sky.

A sundial is a tool that measures time this way. The shadow of the dial points in different directions at different times of day.

Shadows always form on the opposite side of a light source.

The shadows on this sundial help us tell time.

 **Quick Check**

Circle the letter of the correct answer.

11. Look at the photo on page 186. Where is the light coming from?

    a. above the childen

    b. behind the children

    c. in front of the children

What are transparent and translucent materials?

Some objects let light energy pass through them. This lets us see things on the other side.

Transparent objects allow most light energy to pass through. Clear glass and clean water are examples. You can see things on the other side. The light energy reflecting off them passes through the transparent object. Your eyes can take in this energy.

◀ **Light can pass through transparent materials.**

Translucent objects let some light through. Some light is absorbed and some is reflected. This makes it harder to see things on the other side.

Colored glass is an example of a translucent object. Only some light from the other side passes through to reach your eyes.

This window has both transparent and translucent glass.

✔ *Quick Check*

12. Use the graphic organizer below to compare transparent and translucent objects.

Transparent (different)   **Alike**   **Translucent** (different)

Use the vocabulary words on page 171 to fill in the blanks and complete this crossword puzzle

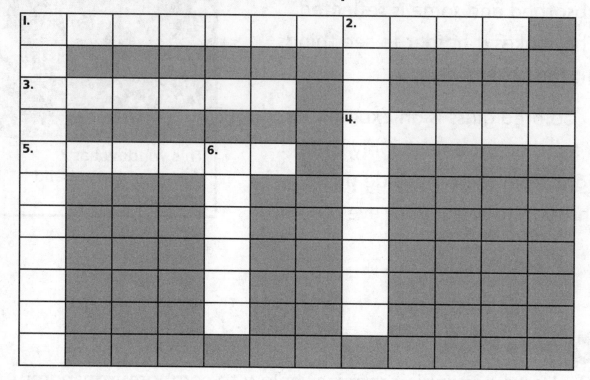

ACROSS

1. Clear glass is _____.

3. A black object will _____ all colors of light.

4. Some _____ waves can turn light skin red or tan.

5. When you block light, you cast a(n) _____.

DOWN

1. Colored glass is _____.

2. A mirror will show your _____.

6. A(n) _____ object will not let light through.

Choose the letter of the correct answer.

1. ____ is a form of energy made of waves.

   a. light
   b. reflection
   c. potential energy
   d. kinetic energy

2. A rough surface does not give a clear ____.

   a. energy
   b. light
   c. shadow
   d. reflection

3. Which colors are absorbed by a red flower?

   a. green
   b. blue
   c. yellow
   d. all of the above

4. An umbrella blocks all light. It is ____.

   a. translucent
   b. opaque
   c. transparent
   d. none of the above

5. When is a shadow formed?

   a. when light passes through an object
   b. when light is absorbed
   c. when light is blocked
   d. when light is reflected

6. Water is an example of a(n) ____.

   a. transparent object
   b. translucent object
   c. opaque object
   d. solid object

Credits